Exodus

Daily Devotions with Jesus

Exodus

Embracing Freedom and Upholding Covenant with God: A Fifty-Day Devotional

GRAHAM JOSEPH HILL

WIPF & STOCK · Eugene, Oregon

EXODUS
Embracing Freedom and Upholding Covenant with God: A Fifty-Day Devotional

Copyright © 2024 Graham Joseph Hill. All rights reserved. Except for brief quotations in critical publications or reviews, no part of this book may be reproduced in any manner without prior written permission from the publisher. Write: Permissions, Wipf and Stock Publishers, 199 W. 8th Ave., Suite 3, Eugene, OR 97401.

Wipf & Stock
An Imprint of Wipf and Stock Publishers
199 W. 8th Ave., Suite 3
Eugene, OR 97401

www.wipfandstock.com

PAPERBACK ISBN: 979-8-3852-1414-3
HARDCOVER ISBN: 979-8-3852-1415-0
EBOOK ISBN: 979-8-3852-1416-7

VERSION NUMBER 03/07/24

"Graham Joseph Hill has produced a devotion that both leads to prayer and to justice—which is just what the book of Exodus does! Hill skillfully invites us to tabernacle with God through Exodus, guiding us into familiarity with the text and wise interpretation."

—**Mark Glanville**, associate professor of pastoral theology, Regent College

"Biblical literacy is essential for people of faith, but such proficiency must lead to a deeper relationship with our God. Graham Joseph Hill's devotional books invite us to comprehend and contemplate biblical texts in ways that are pastorally and personally accessible by the use of daily reflections combined with short podcasts. The goal is deeper faith and discipleship to Jesus."

—**Michael A. Kelly**, CSsR, associate professor of theology, University of Divinity

"If you are searching for a devotional book of daily readings that provides commentary on the context and content of Exodus passages, I recommend reading this book. The readings are brief yet succinctly capture the depth of each chapter. Essential themes of grace, redemption, freedom, justice, and mercy are woven through the text."

—**Lynette Leach**, spiritual director

"It is with great joy that I offer my wholehearted endorsement for this daily devotional. Graham Joseph Hill's deeply insightful reflections take the profound truths of Scripture and present them in a wonderfully helpful, accessible form. This inspiring devotional work is a blessing to me, and I look forward to the subsequent volumes."

—**Nick Scott**, senior pastor, Mount Pleasant Baptist Church

For my daughter, Dakotah.
I adore you
and your compassion, humor,
and care for people.
Every day I thank God for you.
I'm thankful that you're my daughter.

Contents

Introduction | xi

Day 1
Courageous Grace | 1

Day 2
Defiant Faith in Divine Plans | 3

Day 3
Embracing Identity in Christ's Service | 5

Day 4
Heeding the Divine Call | 7

Day 5
Empowered Humility | 9

Day 6
Grace in the Unknown | 11

Day 7
Pathways to Liberation | 13

Day 8
Faithful Catalysts | 15

Day 9
Empowered by Grace | 17

Day 10
Turning Rivers, Transforming Hearts | 19

Day 11
From Resistance to Reconciliation | 21

Day 12
Aligning with Divine Purpose | 23

Day 13
Illuminating the Darkness | 25

Day 14
Reflecting Redemption | 27

Day 15
Living the Passover Promise | 29

Day 16
Grace Unleashed | 31

Day 17
Living Remembrance | 33

Day 18
Navigating Divine Pathways | 35

Day 19
Songs of Deliverance | 37

Day 20
Beyond Bitter Waters | 39

Day 21
Living in Divine Dependence | 41

Day 22
Living Waters in the Desert | 43

Day 23
United in Victory | 45

Day 24
Wisdom in Unity | 47

Day 25
Called to Holiness | 49

Day 26
Pathways of Holiness | 51

Day 27
Justice and Mercy Intertwined | 53

Day 28
Living Justly, Loving Mercy | 55

Day 29
Divine Rhythms of Grace | 57

Day 30
Guided by Grace | 59

Day 31
Covenant Commitment | 61

Day 32
Divine Dwelling Within | 63

Day 33
Sanctuary of the Spirit | 65

Day 34
Living Altars | 67

Day 35
Garments of Grace | 69

Day 36
Sacred Reflections | 71

Day 37
Fragrance of Faith | 73

Day 38
Crafted for Worship | 75

Day 39
Grace Beyond Idols | 77

Day 40
Presence Over Promise | 79

Day 41
Renewed Covenant, Transformed Lives | 81

Day 42
Radiant Reflections | 83

Day 43
United in God's Work | 85

Day 44
Crafting the Kingdom | 87

Day 45
Sacred Craft | 89

Day 46
Sacred Communion | 91

Day 47
Clothed in Holiness | 93

Day 48
Together in Completion | 95

Day 49
Dwelling in Devotion | 97

Day 50
Guided by Glory | 99

Appendix 1
Daily Devotions with Jesus Devotional Books and Podcast | 101

Appendix 2
Bible Reading Plan | 103

Appendix 3
Other Books and Resources by Graham Joseph Hill | 105

Introduction

In the Daily Devotions with Jesus series, Rev. Dr. Graham Joseph Hill guides you through the entire Bible, moving from Genesis to Revelation. Daily Devotions with Jesus podcasts and devotional books show you how each book of the Bible can shape your spiritual life and actions in the world. This is a groundbreaking Bible podcast and devotional book series. See how each book of the Bible deepens your faith and inspires you to follow Jesus in life-changing ways!

In the journey of faith, the book of Exodus is a monumental narrative that reminds us of God's unceasing faithfulness and deliverance. As we embark on this devotional, we are invited to walk alongside the Israelites, witnessing their deliverance from bondage in Egypt to the freedom God ordains for his people.

The Exodus isn't merely a historical recount, but a rich tapestry woven with themes of redemption, law, and God's sovereign power. Here, in the trials and tribulations of the Israelites, we see a reflection of our spiritual sojourn. Much like theirs, our lives often find us in the throes of spiritual deserts, yearning for liberation from the chains of our transgressions and the pursuit of worldly idols.

Through this narrative, we are encouraged to see our own redemption story. Just as the Israelites were led out of Egypt, we, too, are led out of the bondage of sin through the sacrificial love of Christ. The laws given at Sinai, which might seem distant, are a profound expression of God's desire for a holy people, a blueprint for a life of worship and obedience out of gratitude for his grace.

Introduction

As we delve into Exodus, let us allow the Holy Spirit to guide us through the complexities of this ancient text, revealing timeless truths that anchor our faith in the God who saves, provides, and dwells among his people. The journey through Exodus is an inward journey toward a deeper spiritual reality where God's presence transforms us from the inside out.

Dive deep into Exodus. This book invites us into a loving, transformative relationship with Jesus Christ. Through a dedicated fifty-day journey, readers will explore Exodus, unveiling its broader significance within the tapestry of Scripture.

Rooted in rigorous biblical and theological scholarship, this devotional encourages a fuller understanding of the book of Exodus and its relevance in today's world. Each day, readers are invited to meditate on a passage, reflecting on its overarching themes and intricate details. This holistic approach illuminates vital messages often overlooked in cursory or superficial readings.

This daily devotional doesn't shy away from biblical and theological depth. It makes no apology for pushing you to dive deeply into the theological and biblical meanings of the chapters you read. However, this journey isn't merely intellectual. It beckons the heart and spirit, urging readers to engage in intimate conversations with God, share the timeless message of the gospel, and be invigorated toward Christ-glorifying action. Drawing from the ancient narratives, readers will find inspiration to advocate for peace, champion justice, foster reconciliation, extend mercy, and actively partake in society's transformation.

Deep immersion in Scripture invariably leads to a more profound understanding of God's word and its implications for our lives. This devotional, rich with thought-provoking questions and guided prayers, catalyzes a deeper relationship with God. As you turn each page, may you be drawn closer to God's heart and spurred on to walk in the footsteps of Jesus. This journey through Exodus is the third book in a series of devotional books designed to guide you through the entire Bible, nourishing your soul, renewing your purpose, and deepening your theology, contemplation, and action.

INTRODUCTION

Here's what is inside this devotional and how best to use it:

1. The devotional covers the entire book of Exodus over fifty days.
2. Use this book with the Daily Devotions with Jesus podcast—https://grahamjosephhill.com/devotions.
3. Every day as you work your way through this devotional:

    a. *Read* the Bible passage slowly and prayerfully.

    b. *Listen* to the podcast episode for this Bible passage.

    c. *Reflect* on the spiritual devotional.

    d. *Pray* over the Bible passage and devotional and their meanings for your life and the world.

    e. *Act* on your insights.

Reading this Exodus devotional alone, with family, or with a group will help you understand the Bible more fully and put it into practice. Get ready to change.

All Scripture quotations, unless otherwise indicated, are taken from the World English Bible.

Day 1

Courageous Grace

Reading: Exodus 1

In the opening chapter of Exodus, we find ourselves amid a narrative steeped in oppression and the resilience of faith. This chapter, while historical, speaks profoundly to our spiritual lives, guiding us in how to live as Christians in a world that often mirrors the struggles of the Israelites.

The chapter begins with a new Egyptian king who did not know Joseph. This ignorance led to the enslavement and harsh treatment of the Israelites. It's a vivid illustration of how quickly societies can forget the contributions of those who once were esteemed, a reminder of the fleeting nature of worldly recognition and the enduring value of God's providence. Just as the Israelites were oppressed, we, too, can feel burdened by the world's expectations and injustices. Yet, their perseverance under oppression is a testament to the strength that faith in God provides.

This narrative is not just about physical bondage but a spiritual metaphor for the bondage of personal sin. This chapter also highlights the reality of systematic injustice and oppression (including the bondage of consumerism, racism, sexism, classism, and modern slavery). Just as the Israelites were enslaved, we are bound by our personal sins and often by the structural and systemic forces that seek to enslave us. But, like the ancient Israelites, we are not left without hope. This leads us to reflect on the redemptive work of Jesus Christ. He is the greater deliverer, who, unlike Moses, frees us from physical bondage and the spiritual bondage of sin and death. In Jesus, we find the ultimate expression of love, humility, and service. His life, death, and resurrection are the ultimate testament to overcoming oppression, not with force, but with truth-telling, boundary crossing, peacemaking, enemy loving, and sacrificial love.

Moreover, Exodus 1 challenges us to consider our response to the oppressed and marginalized in our society. Are we like the midwives who chose to honor God over the Pharaoh's decree in an act of quiet rebellion? Their courage and faith prompt us to consider how we are called to stand up against injustice and be agents of peace, justice, and reconciliation. It's a call to a gospel-centered life, where our actions and words align in a harmonious testimony to Christ's love and grace.

In living out these themes, we embody the spirit of the gospel. Jesus calls us to love not only our neighbors but also our enemies. To serve others, not as a means to an end, but as an end in itself, reflecting the unconditional love Christ has shown us. Our lives become a living testimony to the grace and compassion of Jesus, a beacon of hope in a world often shrouded in darkness.

Big Idea: Embrace courage and compassion as agents of God's justice and love, reflecting Christ's redemptive grace in a world of oppression.

Reflection: How does the story of the Israelites' oppression and resilience mirror your spiritual journey? In what ways are you called to be an agent of justice and peace in your community, reflecting the love and humility of Christ?

Prayer: Loving God, who hears and liberates us, please guide us in our journey as we navigate the challenges of our world. Help us to find strength in your word, as the Israelites did, and to live out your love in all that we do. May our lives be a testament to your grace as we strive to follow Jesus and embody his teachings in our actions. Amen.

Day 2

Defiant Faith in Divine Plans

Reading: Exodus 2:1-10

In Exodus 2:1-10, we find a profound narrative that intertwines providence, deliverance, and the unfolding of God's plan amid human struggles. This passage, which tells of Moses's birth and early life, is a pivotal point in the biblical story of redemption, offering rich insights into our spiritual journey and God's work in the world.

This passage's heart is the story of a mother's love, a child's deliverance, and God's sovereign hand guiding events for his greater purpose. The faith of Moses's mother, defying the decree of Pharaoh to save her son, speaks volumes about trust in God's protection and provision. This act of defiance is not just a mother's love in action but a profound statement of faith amid adversity.

From a spiritual perspective, Exodus 2:1-10 challenges us to consider our response to God's call, even in the face of seemingly insurmountable challenges. It echoes the need for trust in God's providence and reminds us that our circumstances, however daunting, are never beyond the Spirit's control. The narrative invites us to reflect on how we, like Moses, might be instruments in God's redemptive plan, often in ways we might never anticipate.

Furthermore, this passage has profound implications for how Christians ought to live. It speaks to the themes of justice, compassion, and the courage to stand against oppressive systems. Moses's story begins with an act of civil disobedience, a refusal to comply with an unjust law, setting a tone of resistance against oppression that carries throughout his life. This reminds us of our call to be agents of justice and peace, standing for truth and righteousness in a world marred by sin, deceit, and injustice.

In living out these themes, our focus turns to Jesus. He is the greater Moses, who not only delivers his people from physical bondage but offers eternal salvation and freedom from sin. His life and ministry embodied love, humility, and service to others, setting an example for us to follow. In Christ, we find the enabling grace to live out these principles, to be bearers of peace, beacons of integrity, agents of reconciliation, and communicators of the gospel.

Big Idea: Embrace God's providence by courageously living out justice, compassion, and faith amid life's challenges.

Reflection: How are we responding to God's call in our lives, even when it requires courage and faith amid challenges? How does our life reflect the justice, compassion, and love central to the Christian calling?

Prayer: Almighty One, thank you for the story of Moses and the powerful lessons it teaches us. Help us trust in your providence, be courageous in the face of injustice, and embody Jesus's love and humility daily. May we be instruments of your peace and bearers of your light in this world. Amen.

Day 3

Embracing Identity in Christ's Service

Reading: Exodus 2:11–25

In Exodus 2:11–25, we see a pivotal moment in the life of Moses, a narrative rich with themes that resonate deeply in our spiritual journeys. This passage reveals the complexity of human nature and God's redemptive plan, offering profound insights into how we, as believers, are called to live.

At the heart of this passage is the theme of identity and calling. Moses, raised in Pharaoh's palace yet born a Hebrew, finds himself at a crossroads. His decision to defend a Hebrew against an Egyptian oppressor is more than an act of justice; it is a defining moment of self-identification with his people. Though impulsive and fraught with consequences, this act of solidarity begins Moses's journey toward his God-given destiny.

This narrative prompts us to reflect on our calling and identity in Christ. Like Moses, we are often caught between various identities and loyalties. Our true identity, however, is found in Christ. Jesus calls us to act justly, love mercy, and walk humbly (Micah 6:8), embracing our God-given identity and mission.

Moreover, this passage highlights the theme of seeing and responding to injustice. Moses's reaction to the Egyptian's brutality is immediate and visceral. While his response was flawed, it stemmed from a deep sense of injustice and a desire for change. As followers of Christ, the Spirit calls us to be sensitive to the injustices around us, responding not out of impulsive anger but with Christlike compassion and wisdom. Our actions should be guided by a commitment to integrity, peace, justice, and reconciliation, embodying the gospel in word and deed.

Exodus 2:11–25 also reminds us of the importance of humility and dependence on God. Moses's initial attempt at deliverance fails, leading to a period of exile and refinement. Moses learns to depend on God in the wilderness, preparing him for the monumental task ahead. Similarly, we must recognize our need for God's grace and guidance. No matter how well-intentioned our efforts are, they are futile without God's empowering presence.

Considering Jesus, this passage takes on even greater significance. Christ, the greater Moses, perfectly embodies what Moses could only foreshadow. Jesus identifies with humanity, confronts injustice, and leads us into true freedom through his life, death, and resurrection. We find the ultimate example of love, service, and faithfulness in Jesus Christ. His grace enables us to respond rightly to the challenges and callings of our own lives.

Big Idea: Embrace your identity in Christ to confront injustice with compassionate wisdom and God-dependent humility.

Reflection: How does our identity in Christ shape our response to injustice? Are we seeking God's guidance and strength to live out the gospel?

Prayer: Lord, help us to find our identity in you alone. Give us the courage to stand against injustice, the humility to depend on your strength, and the grace to reflect your love and truth in our lives. Amen.

Day 4

Heeding the Divine Call

Reading: Exodus 3

Exodus 3 presents a transformative moment in the history of redemption, where the narrative of Moses intersects with God's unfolding plan. This chapter, more than a mere historical account, offers profound insights into our spiritual journey and calling as followers of Christ.

In this chapter, Moses encounters the burning bush, a symbol of the God who is holy and transcendent yet imminently present in our world. This divine encounter is not just a call to Moses but also a revelation of God's nature and character. God reveals his name, "I AM," signifying God's eternal, self-existent, and unchanging nature. This revelation invites us to trust in a God who is both beyond our comprehension and intimately involved in our lives.

Exodus 3 speaks powerfully about the nature of the divine calling in our lives. Moses is called to an overwhelming task, yet God assures him, "I will be with you." This promise is foundational for us as believers—our calling, whether grand or humble, is undergirded by the assurance of God's presence. We are never alone in our endeavors for his kingdom. God guides, empowers, and sustains us.

Exodus

The chapter also speaks to themes of humility and obedience. Moses's hesitance and feelings of inadequacy in response to God's call mirror our doubts and fears. Yet, God's call is not based on our ability but on his power and purpose. We are called to respond in obedience and humility, trusting that he who calls us will also equip us.

In the light of the New Testament, this passage points us to Jesus Christ. Just as Moses was called to lead God's people out of bondage, Jesus came to lead humanity out of the bondage of sin and death. Christ embodies God's presence, "I AM," living among us, and through his life, death, and resurrection, he fulfills the ultimate deliverance. In Christ, we find the perfect model of obedience, humility, and sacrificial love.

Exodus 3 challenges us to reflect on our response to God's call. Are we willing to step out in faith, despite our inadequacies, trusting in God's presence, protection, provision, and power? Do we recognize the burning bushes in our lives, moments where God calls us to participate in his redemptive work in the world?

Big Idea: Embrace God's call with humility and trust, recognizing the Spirit of Christ's ever-present power and guidance in our lives.

Reflection: How am I responding to God's call in my life? Am I willing to trust God's presence and power as I engage in Jesus's mission?

Prayer: God of purifying, illuminating, and holy fire, please open our eyes to see your burning bushes, the divine callings you place in our lives. Grant us the humility to accept our inadequacies and the courage to trust in your sufficiency. May we follow you obediently, reflecting the love and grace of Jesus in all that we do. Amen.

Day 5

Empowered Humility

Reading: Exodus 4:1-17

In Exodus 4:1–17, we witness a crucial moment in Moses's life filled with hesitation, self-doubt, and divine reassurance. Moses's reluctance to accept God's call reflects a universal human experience. His objections, "What if they do not believe me?" and "I am not eloquent," mirror our doubts when faced with daunting tasks. This is not just about Moses's story but also our story in our walk with God. The passage teaches us about God's nature, willingness to equip the unequipped, and patience with our frailties.

The signs God provides Moses—the staff turning into a serpent, the leprous hand, and the water turning into blood—are not merely miracles but symbols of God's power and presence. They teach us that in our inadequacies, God's strength is made perfect. When we feel unqualified or unworthy, it is not our ability that matters but our availability to God's calling.

Furthermore, this passage speaks to the essence of Christian living. It's about the courage to confront injustice, as Moses did in Egypt, fueled by the knowledge that God stands with us. It's about humility, recognizing that our abilities are gifts from God meant for service, not self-aggrandizement. In our efforts to promote peace, justice, reconciliation, love, compassion, and the gospel, we find our actions aligned with God's purposes, as Moses did.

The interaction between Moses and Aaron is also instructive. It shows the importance of community and partnership in God's work. We are not meant to bear burdens alone; collaboration and mutual support are vital in our spiritual journey. This teaches us about serving others, loving our neighbors, and even our enemies in the pattern of Christ.

This passage also directs us towards Jesus. Just as Moses was called to deliver Israel, Jesus came as the ultimate deliverer. His life, death, and resurrection embody the ultimate act of love, humility, and service. In Christ, we find the grace and strength to respond to our callings. Jesus is our example in embodying the gospel, communicating it effectively, and living out its implications in our daily lives.

Big Idea: Depend on God's strength in our weakness to fulfill his purpose courageously.

Reflection: How are we responding to God's call in our lives, even in our inadequacies? Are we open to God's enabling power, transforming our weaknesses into strengths for his purpose?

Prayer: Our God, who empowers the weak, thank you for your constant presence in our lives. Please help us to trust in your power and not our own. Guide us to live out the gospel in every aspect of our lives, showing love, humility, and grace. May we, like Moses, be willing vessels for your great purposes. In Jesus's name, amen.

Day 6

Grace in the Unknown

Reading: Exodus 4:18–31

In Exodus 4:18–31, we witness a profound moment in Moses's journey as he heeds God's call to return to Egypt. This passage offers a rich tapestry of themes relevant to our spiritual lives, inviting us to reflect deeply on our own journey of faith.

Firstly, the passage reflects the tension between human hesitancy and divine assurance. Moses, initially reluctant, is reassured by God's presence. This hesitancy mirrors our spiritual lives, where we often encounter God's calling amid our doubts and fears. God's reassurance to Moses reminds us of God's unwavering presence in our lives, especially in moments of uncertainty.

Moreover, the passage emphasizes the importance of obedience and trust in God's plan. Despite his initial reluctance, Moses's return to Egypt signifies a surrender to God's will. This act of obedience is a powerful example for us. The Spirit of Christ often calls us to step out in faith, trusting in God's more excellent plan, even when it seems daunting or unclear.

Exodus 4:18–31 also underscores the theme of transformation. Once a fugitive, Moses is now a chosen leader, demonstrating that God often uses the most unlikely people for divine purposes. This transformation is a testament to God's grace, which works in and through our weaknesses and past failings. It encourages us to see ourselves and others through the lens of God's transformative grace.

Furthermore, this passage points us to Jesus, the ultimate example of obedience, transformation, and God's presence. Jesus, in his earthly ministry, embodied these themes, showing us how to live out our faith. His life and teachings exemplify love, humility, service, and the importance of following God's will. In Jesus, we find the strength and grace to respond to our calling, just as Moses did.

Big Idea: Cherish God's transformative grace to live out your faith courageously amid uncertainty.

Reflection: How is God calling us to step out in faith in our current circumstances? What areas of our lives need to experience God's transforming grace?

Prayer: Our God, you are the God of grace, empowerment, and reassurance in our vulnerability, weakness, and hesitancy. Thank you for the lessons we learn from Moses's journey. Please help us trust your presence and guidance, especially when we face uncertainty or challenges. Grant us the courage to step out in faith, following your will for our lives. Transform us, Lord Jesus, so we may reflect your love and grace to those around us. May this reflection on Exodus 4:18–31 encourage and strengthen our spiritual journey, reminding us of God's unfailing presence and transformative grace. In Jesus's name, amen.

Day 7

Pathways to Liberation

Reading: Exodus 5

Exodus 5, nestled in the saga of Israel's liberation, reveals much about the nature of oppression, the cost of freedom, and the sovereign hand of God in human affairs.

The chapter begins with Moses and Aaron standing before Pharaoh, demanding the release of the Israelites. This bold request is met with scorn and increased oppression as Pharaoh imposes harsher labor on the Israelites. The Israelites, crushed under this added burden, turn against Moses and Aaron. Here, we see a vivid portrayal of how the quest for liberation often meets resistance, externally and internally.

Spiritually, Exodus 5 mirrors our journey. Just as the Israelites yearned for deliverance, our souls long for freedom from the bondage of sin, self, and oppressive systems. Let's begin with internal struggles. This narrative teaches us about the cost of spiritual liberation. Often, when we seek to break free from our spiritual "Pharaohs"—be it pride, addiction, anxiety, or fear—the initial response might be an intensification of struggle. This is a pivotal moment in our spiritual lives where faith is refined. Like the Israelites, the path to freedom is not without its trials.

Moreover, Exodus 5 challenges us to consider how we respond to oppression, suffering, and injustices. Like the Israelites, do we blame or attack those who seek to help us, or do we trust in God's plan, even when it seems counterintuitive? This invites us to cultivate humility, patience, and trust in God's timing and methods. Furthermore, like Moses, do we heed God's call to confront injustice and be agents of Christ's spiritual, physical, and social liberation (vessels of Jesus Christ's holistic freedom and shalom)?

The themes of Exodus 5 also call us to a life of active faith and discipleship. In standing up to Pharaoh, Moses and Aaron exemplify the courage and commitment required to follow God's call. This story mirrors our call to stand against injustice, to be allied with those who have been silenced, and to embody the values of the kingdom of God in a world often resistant to it. The chapter encourages us to engage in acts of peace, justice, liberation, and reconciliation, driven not by our strength but by the enabling grace of God.

The narrative of Exodus 5 points us to Jesus Christ. In Christ, we find the ultimate liberator who, through his love and sacrifice, frees us from the ultimate bondage of sin and death. His life and teachings provide a blueprint for responding to personal and societal challenges, embodying love, service, justice, truth-telling, compassion, and forgiveness.

Big Idea: See trials as pathways to spiritual liberation and active discipleship in Christ's footsteps while waiting on God's deliverance.

Reflection: How do we respond to the trials that accompany our journey toward spiritual freedom? Are we willing to stand for justice and peace, as Christ exemplified, even when it is challenging?

Prayer: God of compassionate presence amid our trials, please help us to trust in your sovereign plan. Grant us the courage to stand against injustice, the humility to accept your timing, and the grace to follow you wholeheartedly. In Jesus's name, amen.

Day 8

Faithful Catalysts

Reading: Exodus 6

In Exodus 6, we encounter a profound moment where God reaffirms God's promises to Israel in their bondage. In verse 5, God says, "I have heard the groaning of the children of Israel, whom the Egyptians keep in bondage, and I have remembered my covenant." This passage resonates deeply with themes of deliverance, promise, and identity—motifs woven through our spiritual lives.

At the heart of Exodus 6 lies the assurance of God's deliverance. Here, God reveals the divine name, Yahweh, underscoring God's faithfulness and unchanging nature. The passage speaks of a God who hears the groaning of God's people and remembers the divine covenant. Our God is not a distant deity, but a profoundly personal God intimately involved in the struggles and liberation of God's people.

This chapter is a resounding echo of hope amid despair. It reminds us that, like Israel, we are not forgotten or abandoned in our struggles. Often marred by spiritual bondage, societal evils, and existential angst, our lives find solace in the promise of God's deliverance. This deliverance, however, is not just an escape from physical or emotional chains; it is an invitation into a relationship with a God who knows us by name.

Exodus 6 also speaks profoundly to how God calls Christians to live. It presents a paradigm of deliverance that goes beyond the individual to a communal, societal level. As followers of Christ, the Spirit calls us to be agents of redemption and deliverance in a world rife with injustice and brokenness. This entails pursuing peace, advocating justice, and embodying reconciliation. It means communicating the gospel in words and actions that reflect Christ's love, humility, and compassion.

Moreover, this chapter challenges us to view our enemies and neighbors through God's redemptive plan. In doing so, Jesus calls us to a radical love that seeks the welfare of others, extending forgiveness and compassion in a manner that reflects the heart of God. Our faith, grounded in the God of Exodus, compels us to serve as the hands and feet of Jesus in a world yearning for hope and healing.

Central to the narrative of Exodus 6 is the foreshadowing of Christ. The deliverance of Israel points us to the ultimate deliverance and salvation achieved through Jesus. In him, the promises of God find their fulfillment. His life, death, and resurrection embody the most profound expressions of God's love, enabling us, his disciples, to respond to the themes of Exodus 6. In Christ, we find the grace to live out the call to love, serve, and witness.

Big Idea: Receive God's faithfulness as a catalyst for living out Jesus Christ's redemptive love in our communities.

Reflection: How does the promise of God's faithfulness in Exodus 6 speak to our current struggles? In what ways are we called to participate in God's redemptive plan in our communities?

Prayer: Faithful and loving God, please remind us of your unchanging promises amid our trials. Grant us the grace to live as reflections of your love, serving as agents of your faith, hope, peace, love, and justice in the world. In Jesus's name, amen.

Day 9

Empowered by Grace

Reading: Exodus 7:1–13

In Exodus 7:1–13, we encounter a pivotal moment in the narrative of Israel's liberation. Here, Moses stands before Pharaoh, emboldened by God to act as God's spokesperson. This passage sets the stage for the ensuing plagues and reveals profound truths about God's sovereignty, human resistance, and the unfolding of divine purposes.

At its heart, this passage teaches us about the power and authority of God. Once a hesitant speaker, Moses is elevated to a position akin to a god before Pharaoh, with Aaron as his prophet. This transformation is a testament to God's ability to empower the unequipped and to exalt the lowly for God's divine purposes. In Pharaoh's stubbornness and the hardening of his heart, we observe a cautionary tale of resistance to God's will, illustrating how human defiance can set the stage for divine demonstration.

This passage challenges us to consider our response to God's calling. It prompts us to reflect on how we might feel inadequate for the tasks God sets before us, like Moses. Yet, the narrative assures us that it is not our ability but God's power through us that accomplishes God's purposes. The resistance of Pharaoh serves as a mirror, urging us to examine areas in our lives where we might be hardening our hearts against God's voice.

In living out these lessons, Jesus calls Christians to a life marked by humility and reliance on God. The transformation of Moses from a fugitive to a leader exemplifies the transformative power of God in our lives. In our pursuit of mercy, compassion, peace, justice, reconciliation, and proclaiming the gospel of salvation, we must remember that these are not merely human endeavors but divine missions. We are encouraged to approach our calling with a heart of service, compassion, and a willingness to be used by God, much like Moses and Aaron.

Furthermore, this passage points us to Jesus. In Moses, we see a foreshadowing of Christ, who came as the ultimate liberator, not from physical bondage but from the bondage of sin and death. Through his life and ministry, Jesus embodied humility, service, and obedience to the Father's will, showing us how to live in response to God's call.

Big Idea: Receive God's power in our inadequacy to fulfill God's transformative purposes in the world.

Reflection: Where might God call us to step out in faith despite our inadequacy? How can we ensure our hearts remain soft and responsive to God's leading?

Prayer: God who empowers the weak and inadequate, thank you for the lessons from Exodus 7:1–13. Help us embrace Moses's humility, obedience to your call, and courage to face the Pharaohs in our lives. May we be instruments of your love, gospel, peace, justice, and reconciliation in a world that desperately needs to see your love in action. Empower us by your grace to be faithful disciples of Jesus, reflecting his love and light in all we do. Amen.

Day 10

Turning Rivers, Transforming Hearts

Reading: Exodus 7:14-25

Exodus 7:14-25 tells the story of the first plague in Egypt, where the Nile turns to blood, a pivotal event that speaks profoundly into our spiritual lives and Christian discipleship. This passage reveals spiritual truths, highlighting the nature of God's power, justice, and the transformative journey of faith.

This passage shows the confrontation between God's sovereignty and human arrogance. Pharaoh, symbolizing the epitome of human rebellion against God's will, faces the divine mandate for liberation. The Nile, the lifeblood of Egypt, turns to blood, a sign of judgment and a disruption of the natural order. This act reminds us that human structures or powers cannot thwart God's purposes.

Spiritually, this narrative invites us to reflect on the areas of our lives where we, like Pharaoh, resist God's authority. It challenges us to consider how we might rely on our own "Niles"—the things we believe sustain us apart from God. The turning of the Nile to blood is a stark reminder that what we often depend on for life can become a source of death when it replaces God in our lives.

Furthermore, the plague narrative in Exodus encourages us to embrace a lifestyle marked by humility, compassion, and a deep sense of justice. The Bible calls Christians to recognize God's authority over all creation and respond obediently and submit. This means actively seeking justice, particularly for those oppressed and marginalized, much like the Israelites in Egypt. Our call to gospel communication is not merely about speaking words of truth but living out a life that embodies God's transformative power and justice.

The themes of Exodus 7 also align with the character of Jesus. Jesus, in his life and ministry, demonstrated the ultimate example of humility, service, and love. He reached out to the marginalized, challenged the powerful, and brought a message of hope and redemption. As his disciples, the Spirit calls us to follow his example, embodying the values of God's upside-down kingdom in a world that often mirrors Pharaoh's Egypt in its rebellion against God.

Big Idea: Seek humble obedience to God, rejecting worldly dependencies to live out God's justice and love.

Reflection: How are we resisting God's authority in our lives? What are the "Niles" we depend on instead of God? How can we more faithfully embody Jesus's example of love, service, compassion, and justice daily?

Prayer: Divine Creator, who turned the Nile to blood and liberated your people, guide us in understanding the depths of your power and justice. Please help us identify and relinquish our resistance to your will. May we walk in the footsteps of Jesus, embodying your love and justice in our world. Empower us by your grace to be faithful disciples, reflecting your transformative love to those around us. Amen.

Day 11

From Resistance to Reconciliation

Reading: Exodus 8

Exodus 8 presents a narrative rich in symbolism and spiritual depth, inviting us to explore its implications for our spiritual lives and Christian discipleship.

At its core, Exodus 8 depicts a series of plagues, each a demonstration of God's power over the Egyptian gods and a call to Pharaoh to release the Israelites. These events carry deep spiritual meanings. They signify the supremacy of God over all earthly powers and the futility of human pride and stubbornness. The plagues, particularly the invasion of frogs, gnats, and flies, symbolize the chaos and disorder that ensue when humanity chooses to live independently of the divine will.

This chapter speaks directly to our spiritual lives today. It reminds us that, like Pharaoh, we often resist God's call, clinging to our control and comfort. The plagues, therefore, can be seen as metaphors for the internal turmoil and spiritual disarray we experience when we turn away from God's path. We often face unnecessary hardships in our resistance, much like the Egyptians did. This narrative invites us to reflect on areas where we might resist God's guidance, urging us to relinquish our control and trust in the divine plan.

Furthermore, Exodus 8 calls Christians to a life characterized by peace, justice, and humility. The plagues demonstrate the consequences of arrogance and the abuse of power. As followers of Christ, we are called to embody the opposite spirit—one of service, compassion, and love for neighbors, strangers, fellow believers, and enemies. This chapter challenges us to consider how we might contribute to the "plagues" and brokenness in our communities through indifference or inaction and calls us to be ambassadors of the gospel of salvation. This gospel leads us to prioritize justice, liberation, mercy, inclusion, love, compassion, and reconciliation.

Love, humility, and service don't always transform resistance to Christ and his kingdom into life-giving reconciliation—but they often do.

The narrative of Exodus 8 also points us toward Jesus. In Christ, we see the ultimate example of humility and service, someone who submitted entirely to God's will, unlike Pharaoh. Jesus embodies the deliverance that the Israelites longed for, offering freedom not just from physical bondage and oppression but from the bondage of sin and death. His life and teachings provide the grace and strength we need to respond to the challenges and themes presented in Exodus 8.

Big Idea: Embrace humility and service, embodying Christ's love, and, in doing so, join with Jesus in transforming pain into healing and resistance into reconciliation.

Reflection: Where are we resisting God's call in our lives, and how can we embrace a posture of humility and service? Through Christ's example, how can we be agents of peace and reconciliation in our communities?

Prayer: Divine Guide, in the complexities of our lives, help us see your hand at work. Teach us to trust in your plan, to relinquish our control, and to walk humbly in your ways. Inspired by Jesus's example, may we be instruments of your peace and love in a world often marred by pride and discord. Amen.

Day 12

Aligning with Divine Purpose

Reading: Exodus 9

Exodus 9 presents a profound exploration of God's sovereignty and mercy, human stubbornness, our propensity to dehumanize those who are different from us, and the consequences of sin. This chapter, nestled in the narrative of Israel's deliverance from Egypt, speaks volumes about the nature of divine intervention and human hearts and responses.

At its core, Exodus 9 illustrates the tension between God's unyielding will and Pharaoh's hardened heart. Here, we see a clear depiction of God's power over creation, as evidenced through the plagues, and yet there is also an undeniable emphasis on human responsibility and choice. This duality invites us to reflect deeply on the nature of God's interaction with the world and our response to divine directives.

Exodus 9 serves as a mirror, reflecting our tendencies to resist God's will. "The heart of Pharaoh was hardened . . ." (v. 35). Like Pharaoh, we often battle wills with the Divine, clinging to our plans and desires. Our hearts can become hard to God's will and the humanity of those different from us. This resistance, as illustrated in Exodus, leads to suffering and chaos for us and those around us. When we dehumanize others and collude in or ignore their suffering, our hearts become hard toward God and our fellow human beings. In contrast, though challenging, asking the Spirit for a soft heart and submitting to God's will brings liberation and aligns us with a purpose greater than our own.

The narrative of Exodus 9 also calls Christians to embody values like compassion, justice, and humility. As we witness the destruction brought by the plagues, our hearts are moved towards a deeper understanding of suffering and the importance of aligning ourselves with God's heart for the oppressed and marginalized. This alignment requires an active pursuit of peace, reconciliation, and service to others, embodying the love and humility of Christ in our daily interactions.

Furthermore, Exodus 9 points us to Jesus, the ultimate embodiment of God's grace and love. In Christ, we see the fulfillment of God's promise of deliverance, not only from physical bondage and oppressive systems and structures but from the bondage of sin and death. Through Jesus, we receive the strength and grace needed to respond to life's challenges and to live out the themes of justice, compassion, and love demonstrated throughout Exodus.

Big Idea: Pursue God's will with humility and compassion to manifest justice, peace, and Christ's love in our world.

Reflection: How are we resisting God's will in our own lives, and what are the consequences of this resistance? How can we more actively pursue justice, compassion, and service in our daily lives, reflecting the heart of Jesus?

Prayer: Dear Lord, grant us the wisdom to discern your will and the courage to follow it. Help us to embody your love and grace in our actions, seeking justice, showing compassion, and serving those around us. May we reflect the light of Christ in all that we do. Amen.

Day 13

Illuminating the Darkness

Reading: Exodus 10

Exodus 10 presents a profound narrative that intertwines divine justice, human stubbornness, and the transformative power of God's intervention in the world. This chapter, in which God sends a plague of locusts and darkness over Egypt, is a spiritual mirror reflecting the depths of human rebellion and God's unwavering commitment to liberation and righteousness.

The locusts and darkness in Exodus 10 are not merely physical calamities but serve as metaphors for spiritual blindness and the devastating consequences of sin. Like Pharaoh, our hearts can become hardened, resistant to God's voice. This hardening leads to a life shrouded in spiritual darkness, where the richness and beauty of God's creation, much like the fertile land of Egypt, is devoured by our insatiable egos and desires.

However, the narrative of Exodus is not one of despair but of hope and redemption. God's actions are not merely punitive but are also redemptive. They reveal a God who is deeply involved in the world's affairs, hears the cries of the oppressed, and acts decisively to liberate them. In this light, the plagues demonstrate God's power and a call to humility, repentance, and faith.

Exodus 10 challenges us to reflect on our resistance to God's will. Are there areas in our lives where we have hardened our hearts? The plagues remind us that our actions have consequences for ourselves and the world around us. They are a call to humility and self-examination. The Spirit of Jesus calls us to turn away from our self-centered ways and to embrace a life of faith and obedience to God.

This chapter also informs how we, as Christians, should live. It calls us to be ambassadors of integrity, humility, and justice in a world often marked by the opposite. The darkness of the plague can be seen as a metaphor for the darkness of injustice and oppression that pervades society. As followers of Jesus Christ, we are called to bring light into these dark places, to stand with the marginalized and oppressed, to oppose dehumanizing forces, and to work tirelessly for a world that reflects God's justice and love.

In doing so, we point to Jesus, the ultimate liberator, who conquered the powers of sin and death through his life, death, and resurrection. Jesus's example teaches us the importance of humility and compassion. His love empowers us to be disciples with humble and soft hearts who live out these values daily.

Big Idea: Cultivate transformative faith by actively seeking to bring light into the world's darkness, following Christ's example of justice and compassion.

Reflection: In what ways have we experienced spiritual blindness, and how can we open our eyes to God's truth? How can we, as disciples of Christ, bring light into the dark places of our world?

Prayer: Lord of Holy and Loving Light, who brought light out of darkness and order out of chaos, please guide our hearts to see your truth. Help us to turn away from our sinful ways and embrace a life of love, humility, and obedience to your will. Empower us by your Spirit to be agents of peace and justice in a world that needs your transformative love. Amen.

Day 14

Reflecting Redemption

Reading: Exodus 11

In the heart of Exodus 11, we find a profound narrative that speaks to the depths of our spiritual journey. This passage, rich in symbolism and historical significance, presents the final plague in Egypt—a moment of judgment and deliverance. It's a story that recounts a pivotal moment in Israel's history and offers timeless insights into our spiritual lives.

The plague on the firstborn is a terrifying and disturbing story. However, at its core, Exodus 11 is a testament to God's sovereignty and justice. The impending plague, the death of the firstborn in Egypt, serves as a decisive act demonstrating that no earthly power, not even Pharaoh, stands above the divine. This account reminds us that God hears the cries of the oppressed and acts to deliver them, showcasing both God's mercy for the Israelites and judgment against the oppressors.

We are living in an age of dictators, autocrats, tycoons, tyrants, and oppressors. But Exodus reminds us that our Lord God is sovereign over history, peoples, and powers, and God's righteousness, freedom, sovereignty, and justice will have the final say.

For our spiritual lives, Exodus 11 offers a powerful mirror. It reminds us of the stark contrast between the ways of the world, represented by Pharaoh's hard-heartedness, and the ways of God, marked by justice, mercy, and deliverance. As followers of Jesus Christ, his Spirit calls us to recognize and resist the "Pharaohs" of our time—the systemic injustices, personal sins, and religious and societal structures that enslave and oppress. In doing so, we align ourselves with God's redemptive work.

Furthermore, the narrative of Exodus 11 propels us towards a life marked by compassion, justice, and humility. In the face of injustice, we are called not to the vengeance of the world but to the restorative justice of God. We are to be agents of peace and reconciliation, embodying Christ's love and humility in our interactions with others, including our neighbors and enemies. The Bible urges us to rely on God's fearsome and holy power and justice while also serving others selflessly, extending forgiveness and compassion as we reflect the heart of God in our communities.

Exodus 11 points us to Jesus. The deliverance of Israel prefigures the ultimate salvation brought by Christ. Jesus embodies the fullness of God's love, grace, and mercy, offering himself as the ultimate sacrifice for our redemption. In Jesus Christ, we find the strength to live out the themes of Exodus 11 and the rest of Scripture—to trust God's power and righteousness while pursuing justice, showing mercy, and walking humbly with our God.

Big Idea: Pursue God's justice and mercy daily as reflections of Christ's redemptive love.

Reflection: How am I embodying God's justice and mercy daily? In what ways am I resisting the "Pharaohs" of this age and aligning myself with God's redemptive work?

Prayer: Gracious God, as we meditate on Exodus 11, instill in us a heart that seeks justice, loves mercy, and walks humbly with you. Empower us through your Spirit to be agents of your redemptive love. Guide us to live in the example of Jesus, showing compassion, forgiveness, and grace to all. Amen.

Day 15

Living the Passover Promise

Reading: Exodus 12:1-30

In the heart of Exodus 12:1-30, we find a narrative brimming with spiritual significance, a passage that speaks to the depth of our faith journey. This Scripture, chronicling the first Passover, is not merely a historical account but a rich tapestry, weaving together themes of deliverance, sacrifice, and divine providence.

The Passover event is a profound illustration of God's redemptive plan. The lamb's blood painted on the doorposts symbolizes salvation. It points to a deeper truth: the necessity of a substitute to bear the weight of judgment. This act of protection and provision mirrors our spiritual journey, where we are shielded not by our merits but by the grace extended to us.

In our spiritual lives, Exodus 12 serves as a reminder of the radical nature of God's intervention. It challenges us to reflect on the extent of divine grace that covers our flaws and redeems our stories. The Passover lamb prefigures the ultimate sacrifice, leading us to contemplate Christ's profound love and sacrifice. It's a call to embrace a faith not grounded in ritual or tradition but in a living, breathing relationship with the Divine.

This narrative also speaks profoundly to how we should live as followers of Christ. The themes of liberation and justice woven into the Exodus story urge us to be agents of peace and reconciliation in a fractured world. It beckons us to a life of humble service, reflecting the sacrificial love of the Passover lamb in our interactions with neighbors, strangers, adversaries, and fellow Christians. Our actions and words become conduits of grace, mirroring the compassion and forgiveness we've received.

Moreover, Exodus 12:1–30 calls us to a life of active faith and witness. Just as the Israelites were to recount the story of Passover to future generations, we, too, are called to bear witness to the transformative power of God's love in our lives. This witnessing is not a passive act but an active living out of the gospel principles of love, service, and justice.

In reflecting on this passage, we see a clear pointer to Jesus. The Passover lamb prefigures Christ's ultimate sacrifice, embodying the fullest expression of divine love and grace. It's in Jesus that we find the strength to live out the themes of Exodus 12. What are those themes? This passage invites us to trust God's deliverance and redemption, sovereignty and power, judgment and mercy, providence and protection, and substitution and sacrifice. The communal aspect of the Passover meal relates to its role in forming a collective identity for God's people.

By God's grace alone and through the sacrifice of Jesus, God's people are set apart and chosen by God. These chosen people can live out the Passover promise of hope, redemption, and new life and be a shining light to the world.

Big Idea: Choose a life of sacrificial love and active faith, reflecting God's redemptive grace in every action and relationship.

Reflection: How am I living out the principles of love, sacrifice, and redemption daily? Am I a conduit of God's grace to those around me?

Prayer: Divine Shepherd, thank you for the gift of your grace and the example of sacrificial love shown in Exodus. Help us to internalize these truths and live them out in our daily walk with you. May our lives be a testament to your love and redemption. May we be ever grateful for your Son, the divine sacrificial Lamb, and glorify him in our hearts, words, and actions. Amen.

Day 16

Grace Unleashed

Reading: Exodus 12:31-51

In Exodus 12:31-51, we witness the climax of the Israelites' deliverance from Egypt, a pivotal moment that intertwines liberation, identity, and divine providence.

The exodus from Egypt symbolizes a journey from bondage to freedom, a theme that resonates deeply with the Christian experience. The Passover, introduced in these verses, is more than an ancient ritual; it foreshadows the ultimate sacrifice made by Christ. Just as the Israelites marked their doorposts with the blood of a lamb for physical salvation, we, too, are marked by the blood of Christ for spiritual salvation. This deliverance is physical liberation and a holistic transformation encompassing social, political, and spiritual realms.

Exodus 12:31-51 offers a compelling narrative of faith and obedience for our spiritual lives. As the Israelites trusted God's instructions, we are called to trust God's provision and guidance, even amid uncertainty and peril. This passage beckons us to recognize the power of God's grace in our lives, which frees us from the bondage of sin and guides us into a life of discipleship and service.

In response to this passage, Christians are called to live out values that reflect the heart of the exodus story. The themes of justice, reconciliation, and humility emerge as crucial elements in this narrative. Just as the Israelites were freed from oppression, we are called to be agents of justice, working towards the liberation and well-being of those who are marginalized and oppressed. The story of the exodus challenges us to embrace a life of humility, recognizing that our freedom is not a result of our efforts but a gift of divine grace.

Moreover, Exodus 12:31–51 calls us to a life of radical love and service. God frees us to be beacons of righteousness, justice, and love. Such love is not a passive emotion but an active commitment to the welfare of others, including our neighbors and enemies. This kind of love mirrors the sacrificial love of Christ, who laid down his life for the sake of the world.

As we reflect on this passage, it points us unmistakably to Jesus. We see the perfect embodiment of liberation, sacrifice, and love in him. His life, death, and resurrection are the ultimate fulfillment of the exodus story, offering us a model to follow and the grace and strength to live out these truths daily.

Big Idea: Embrace God's liberating grace in Christ to actively pursue justice, love, and humble service daily.

Reflection: How does understanding the exodus story deepen your appreciation of Christ's sacrifice? In what ways are you called to embody the values of liberation, justice, and love in your community?

Prayer: Loving God, thank you for the gift of liberation and life we find in your word and in your Son, Jesus Christ. Help us to grasp the depth of your love and grace and empower us to live as vessels of your justice, peace, and love in the world. Amen.

Day 17

Living Remembrance

Reading: Exodus 13:1-16

Exodus 13:1-16, a passage rich in symbolism and meaning, is a powerful reminder of God's deliverance and the importance of remembrance in our spiritual journey. While deeply rooted in the historical context of the Israelites' exodus from Egypt, this passage transcends time and space to speak into our lives today.

At its core, Exodus 13:1-16 emphasizes the significance of consecration and remembrance. The Israelites are instructed to dedicate their firstborn to God as a continual reminder of their deliverance from bondage in Egypt. This act of consecration is not just a ritual. It's a profound expression of gratitude and acknowledgment of God's mighty hand in their lives. Similarly, in our spiritual walk, we are called to remember and dedicate our lives to God, recognizing the freedom we have been granted from the bondage of sin and death.This act of remembrance is crucial, for it roots us in our identity as God's beloved and reminds us of the grace that sustains us.

Delving deeper, this passage also speaks to themes of justice, service, and humility. The Israelites' deliverance was not merely for their benefit but was part of a larger narrative of God's justice and mercy. As modern believers, we are called to embody these same values. This means actively working towards peace and reconciliation in our communities, showing love and compassion to our neighbors and enemies, and humbly serving others in Christ's love. These actions are not just moral obligations but expressions of gratitude for God's deliverance in our lives.

Moreover, Exodus 13:1–16 challenges us to reflect on the nature of our witness. How do our lives testify to the grace and love we have received? Are we living examples of God's transformative power, or are we merely going through the motions? This passage invites us to reevaluate our priorities and align them with God's call to love, serve, and witness to the gospel.

Considering all this, we see a clear connection to Jesus. He is the ultimate embodiment of God's deliverance, grace, and love. His life, death, and resurrection fulfill the liberation foreshadowed in the Exodus narrative. In Jesus, we find the strength and grace to live out the themes of Exodus 13:1–16. His example inspires us to pursue justice, love mercy, and walk humbly with God—to be a people shining with Christ's faith, hope, and love.

Big Idea: Develop a life of gratitude and service, embodying God's deliverance and love in every action.

Reflection: How am I living out the values of justice, service, and humility in my daily life? How does my life bear witness to the deliverance and grace I have received in Christ?

Prayer: Gracious God, thank you for the freedom and deliverance you have granted us through your mighty hand. Please help us to remember your deeds and dedicate our lives to you. Empower us by your grace to live out your call to justice, service, and humility, following the example of your Son, Jesus Christ. Amen.

Day 18

Navigating Divine Pathways

Reading: Exodus 13:17—14:31

This passage is a vivid portrayal of deliverance. The Israelites, led by Moses, are escaping the bondage of Egypt, symbolizing the liberation from the enslavement of sin, bondage, and darkness. As they journey towards the Red Sea, their path seems impossible. Yet, the waters parting signifies the omnipotent power of God to make a way where there seems to be none. This miraculous event is a testament to the truth that divine intervention can lead us to freedom and victory when we face seemingly insurmountable challenges.

Spiritually, this passage speaks profoundly to our journey of faith. It reminds us that our walk with God often takes us through unexpected routes, where our faith is tested and refined. The Israelites' journey through the wilderness, away from the direct route to Canaan, symbolizes the often circuitous path of spiritual growth, where trust in God's timing and wisdom is paramount. This story encourages us to embrace the wilderness seasons as opportunities for deepening our reliance on the Divine.

Furthermore, Exodus 13:17—14:31 challenges us to live out our faith in tangible ways. It calls us to embody principles of peace, justice, and reconciliation, reflecting the character of God in our interactions with others. As the Israelites stood at the edge of the

Red Sea, they faced fear and uncertainty, much like we do in confronting injustices and conflicts in our world. Their story urges us to persevere in faith while advocating for peace and justice and to trust in God's power to bring about transformation in seemingly hopeless situations.

This passage also points to Jesus, the embodiment of divine love and grace. Just as the Israelites were led through the Red Sea to freedom, Jesus leads us through the waters of baptism into a new life of discipleship and service. His life and teachings illuminate the path of loving our neighbors, serving others selflessly, and embodying compassion and forgiveness. In Christ, we find the strength and grace to respond to life's challenges and opportunities with faith and hope.

Big Idea: See God's unexpected pathways as opportunities for faith-driven transformation and service.

Reflection: How are we experiencing God's guidance in our "wilderness" journeys? In what ways are we called to be agents of peace and justice in our communities?

Prayer: Divine Guide, lead us through the complexities of life with your wisdom and strength. Help us trust your timing and plan and empower us to live out your principles of love, liberation, truth-telling, justice, and peace. May we reflect your love and grace to those around us. Amen.

Day 19

Songs of Deliverance

Reading: Exodus 15:1–21

In Exodus 15:1–21, we witness a profound moment of triumph and worship as the Israelites celebrate their deliverance from Egypt. This passage, often called the Song of the Sea, is a vibrant tapestry of thanksgiving, awe, and prophetic hope. It serves as a beacon, guiding us in understanding our spiritual journey and how we are called to live as followers of Christ.

The narrative of Exodus 15 symbolizes a profound spiritual truth. It represents the transformative journey from bondage to freedom, a theme central to the Christian faith. The Israelites' song of deliverance mirrors our journey from the enslavement of sin to the freedom found in Christ. This passage underscores the power of God's deliverance and the subsequent response of worship and trust.

What does this mean for our spiritual lives? The Song of the Sea invites us to reflect on God's saving acts in our own lives. Just as the Israelites sang of the Lord's strength and salvation, we are called to recognize and celebrate God's redemptive work through Jesus Christ. This celebration is not passive but an active response of faith, trust, and gratitude.

Exodus 15:1–21 also speaks powerfully about how Christians should live. The song is not just a reflection of past deliverance but a forward-looking proclamation of hope. In the same way, our lives should be testimonies of God's ongoing work, marked by peace, justice, and reconciliation. The themes of deliverance and salvation should propel us towards active engagement with the world, embodying Christ's love, humility, and compassion. We are called to be agents of peace and reconciliation, reflecting God's justice in our communities and our relationships with neighbors and adversaries.

Moreover, this passage challenges us to embrace the gospel's transformative power. As followers of Jesus, we are called to a life of service, to exhibit a faith that acts in love, and to offer forgiveness as freely as we have received it. Our witness to Christ is authenticated when we live out these values, showing the world a glimpse of God's kingdom.

Considering Exodus 15, how does this point us to Jesus? Jesus embodies the ultimate act of deliverance, freeing us from sin and death. His life, death, and resurrection are the greatest testament to God's love and power. In Jesus, we find the grace and strength to respond to life's challenges and to live out the themes of Exodus 15.

Big Idea: Embrace and proclaim God's transformative deliverance as a testament to God's enduring love and power.

Reflection: How do we see God's deliverance at work in our own lives? How does this awareness shape our response to God and others?

Prayer: O God, who delivered Israel at the Red Sea, guide us in our faith journey. Help us to recognize your hand in our lives and empower us to live in a way that reflects your love and justice. May our lives be songs of praise to you, echoing the hope and freedom we find in Jesus Christ. Amen.

Day 20

Beyond Bitter Waters

Reading: Exodus 15:22-27

In Exodus 15:22-27, we find the Israelites journeying through the wilderness of Shur, where they encounter the bitter waters of Marah. This narrative is not just a mere historical account but a profound spiritual metaphor that resonates deeply with our faith journey today.

At the heart of this passage lies the profound truth of God's provision and guidance, even in the most desolate circumstances. Having just experienced the miraculous deliverance at the Red Sea, the Israelites now face a new challenge: the bitterness of Marah's waters. This stark contrast from triumph to trial reflects our spiritual walk. After experiencing spiritual highs, we often find ourselves in the wilderness, grappling with bitterness and disappointment.

What does this passage mean for our spiritual lives? The story of Marah teaches us about the nature of God's providence and our response to it. Through God's intervention, transforming the bitter waters into sweet symbolizes God's transformative power in our lives. It reminds us that God is still present in our moments of bitterness and trial, working to bring forth sweetness and growth.

Furthermore, the passage provides a blueprint for how Christians should live. We must demonstrate faith, trust in God's provision, and patience in life's challenges. The reaction of the Israelites to their circumstances serves as a reminder that our attitude in times of hardship is crucial. We are called to be people of peace, showing humility and compassion even when circumstances are less than ideal. This narrative encourages us to serve others, maintaining a posture of love and forgiveness, mirroring the character of Christ.

Exodus 15:22–27 also points to Jesus, the ultimate source of transformation and healing. Just as God guided the Israelites to the healing waters, Jesus offers us living water, promising renewal and restoration. In Jesus, we find the grace to navigate our wilderness experiences, the strength to transform our bitterness into growth, and the hope for a future filled with his goodness.

Big Idea: Trust in God's transformative power to turn life's bitterness into opportunities for growth and renewal.

Reflection: How do we respond to the "bitter waters" in our lives? Are we willing to trust in God's transformative power during challenging times?

Prayer: O God, our Guide, and Provider, in our moments of bitterness and trial, help us to trust in your transformative power. Grant us the grace to see your hand at work, turning our trials into testimonies of your faithfulness. May our lives reflect your love and grace as we journey through our wilderness, following the example of Jesus Christ. Amen.

Day 21

Living in Divine Dependence

Reading: Exodus 16

The Israelites, newly freed from Egyptian bondage, find themselves grappling with the harsh realities of the wilderness. Their hunger in the wilderness and God's provision of manna represent a pivotal lesson. This daily bread, appearing each morning, was more than mere sustenance; it was a testament to God's unwavering faithfulness. The manna was not just food but a daily reminder of dependence on God.

In our lives, too, we often encounter wilderness periods—times of uncertainty, waiting, and apparent scarcity. Yet, just as God provided for the Israelites, God provides for us, often unexpectedly. This story invites us to reflect on our reliance on God's provision, challenging us to trust in divine faithfulness, even when the path ahead seems unclear.

Moreover, the story of Exodus 16 is a narrative of learning and unlearning. The Israelites had to unlearn the mentality of scarcity they had known in Egypt and embrace a new mindset of reliance on God. This process mirrors our spiritual journey, where we must unlearn patterns of self-reliance and learn to depend on God's grace. It speaks to the transformative power of grace in shaping our lives, guiding us to live in a way that reflects divine love and justice.

Exodus 16 also speaks profoundly to our call to live out the gospel. The manna was not only a gift but also a responsibility. The Israelites were instructed to gather only as much as they needed, a principle that extends to our understanding of justice and community. In a world marked by excess and inequality, this story urges us to consider how we use resources, calling us to a life of simplicity, sharing, and care of people in need. It's a poignant reminder of our responsibility to love our neighbors and enemies alike, extending compassion, hospitality, generosity, and forgiveness, just as we receive these abundantly from God.

In the figure of Moses, we also see a model of humble leadership, pointing us toward the ultimate example of humility and service—Jesus Christ. Jesus, the true bread from heaven, embodies God's provision and presence. Just as the manna sustained the Israelites, Jesus sustains us on our journey, offering grace that empowers us to respond to life's challenges. His life and teachings illuminate the path of discipleship, guiding us in love, service, and the pursuit of peace and reconciliation.

Big Idea: Grow into daily dependence on God's provision to live a life of humility, justice, and grace.

Reflection: How do we experience God's provision in our wilderness moments? How does this story challenge us to live out the values of the kingdom of God in our daily lives?

Prayer: Eternal Provider, guide us in our wilderness, teach us to trust in your provision, and shape our lives in the image of your Son, Jesus Christ. Amen.

Day 22

Living Waters in the Desert

Reading: Exodus 17:1-7

The narrative of Exodus 17:1-7, woven with themes of doubt, provision, and divine presence, unfolds as the Israelites, weary and thirsty, confront Moses about their lack of water. Their cries, echoing our spiritual thirst, point us toward a deeper understanding of faith and dependence on God.

At the heart of this passage is the Israelites' struggle with trust. Desperate, they question, "Is Yahweh among us, or not?" This query mirrors our doubts in times of need. The Israelites' doubt isn't just about physical thirst; it symbolizes a spiritual drought, a shared experience in our faith walk. How often do we question God's presence and provision when faced with life's trials?

Yet, in God's response through Moses striking the rock at Horeb, we see a vivid illustration of divine provision and grace. God doesn't chastise their doubts but meets their needs by outpouring life-sustaining water. This act is a powerful metaphor for God's grace, constantly flowing and meeting us at our point of need, even when we falter in faith.

In reflecting on this narrative, we are invited to consider our response to life's deserts. Like the Israelites, we may find ourselves in barren places, thirsting for something more. How do we react?

Do we grumble and doubt or turn to God, trusting in divine provision? This passage calls us to a posture of dependence and faith, reminding us that God is always present, even in our driest moments.

Moreover, this story is not just about individual faith but also about community. The Israelites' journey through the desert was a communal experience, reflecting our shared spiritual journey. In our modern context, this passage challenges us to consider how we support each other during spiritual drought. Are we, like Moses, instruments of God's grace to others? Do we offer the water of encouragement, prayer, and practical support to those around us who are struggling?

Turning to Jesus, we see this theme of living water embodied. Christ, the true Rock struck for our sakes, provides a never-ending source of spiritual nourishment. Our deepest thirsts are quenched in Jesus, and our souls find rest. Jesus embodies God's grace, inviting us into discipleship characterized by trust, dependence, and the outpouring of love to others.

Big Idea: Trust in God's provision and be channels of his grace in times of spiritual drought.

Reflection: How is God calling us to trust more deeply in times of need? In what ways are we called to be channels of God's grace to those around us?

Prayer: Divine Provider, who quenches our deepest thirsts, guide us in our moments of doubt and need. Please help us to trust in your constant presence and provision. Empower us to be your hands and feet, sharing your living water with those who thirst. In Jesus's name, amen.

Day 23

United in Victory

Reading: Exodus 17:8-16

Exodus 17:8-16 recounts a momentous battle where Israel, under Moses's leadership, confronts Amalek. Here, we see a vivid tableau of struggle, support, and victory that profoundly impacts our spiritual journey.

The narrative unfolds with Israel at war. Israel prevails as Moses lifts his hands, but when he lowers them, Amalek gains ground. Aaron and Hur provide crucial support by holding up Moses's arms, leading to a decisive victory. More than a historical record, this account is a rich tapestry of spiritual truths, revealing the necessity of communal support, persistent faith, and divine reliance.

This passage is a vivid metaphor for our battles in our spiritual lives. Just as Moses relied on Aaron and Hur, the Bible calls us to lean on and uplift one another. Our faith journey isn't solitary. It's a shared pilgrimage where the burdens and joys are distributed among the community. This narrative also underscores the continuous nature of faith. Just as Moses's arms needed to be upheld, our faith requires constant nurturing and support. It's a dynamic, living process rather than a one-time event.

The battle against Amalek is not merely a physical confrontation but a spiritual allegory. It teaches us about the importance of steadfastness and reliance on the divine. In our struggles, be they moral, spiritual, or physical, the victory comes not from our strength but through perseverance and heavenly aid. Our lifted hands in prayer symbolize our total dependence on the divine, acknowledging that the source of our strength lies beyond ourselves.

Exodus 17:8–16 is a clarion call to embody peace, justice, reconciliation, and the gospel of Jesus Christ. In the face of conflict, the Bible reminds us that our battle is not against flesh and blood but against the powers that seek to divide and destroy. Our response should be one of love, humility, and service, reflecting the character of Jesus. Christ calls us to love our neighbors, enemies, and fellow believers, engaging in radical compassion and forgiveness that mirror divine love.

This narrative points us directly to Jesus. He is our Moses, interceding on our behalf, and our Aaron and Hur, providing the support we desperately need. In Jesus, we find the perfect embodiment of love, humility, and service. His life, death, and resurrection are the ultimate victory over the forces of sin and death. Through Jesus Christ, we are empowered to respond to life's battles with faith, perseverance, and hope.

Big Idea: Develop persistent faith and communal support as the foundation for overcoming life's battles and embodying Christ's love.

Reflection: How can you support others in their spiritual battles? In what areas of your life do you need to rely more fully on divine strength?

Prayer: Divine Shepherd, please be our strength and shield in our battles. Help us to uphold one another in love and to rest in your enduring victory. May our lives reflect your faith, hope, perseverance, and love, and may we walk in the humility and service of Jesus. Amen.

Day 24

Wisdom in Unity

Reading: Exodus 18

In Exodus 18, Moses reunites with his father-in-law, Jethro, who observes the weight of Moses' responsibilities and advises him to delegate authority to capable leaders. This narrative is not merely a lesson in leadership but a profound reflection on the themes of guidance, stewardship, and communal support.

The text suggests that Exodus 18 is about more than administrative wisdom; it's a theological statement about God's desire for order, justice, and shared burden within the community. The appointment of leaders among the Israelites isn't just a practical solution but a divine strategy to cultivate a society rooted in mutual respect and accountability. Here, we see a model of governance that values wisdom, experience, and godly character, reflecting a broader divine order.

Spiritually, Exodus 18 challenges us to consider our roles within our communities and the broader tapestry of God's kingdom. It speaks to the heart of what it means to bear each other's burdens and to lead with humility and discernment. Just as Moses listened to Jethro's counsel, we are reminded of the importance of seeking wisdom from those God places in our lives. This humility is not a sign of weakness but a testament to our reliance on God and each other.

Exodus 18 calls Christians to a different standard of interconnectedness and shared responsibility in a world marred by individualism and isolation. It invites us to live out values of peace, justice, and reconciliation in tangible ways. By distributing tasks and authority, Moses models a leadership that is not about amassing power but empowering others. This reflects a profound truth about God's kingdom, where the last are first, and the greatest are those who serve.

Moreover, Exodus 18 points us to Jesus, the ultimate servant leader. In Christ, we find the perfect embodiment of wisdom, humility, and love. His life and ministry demonstrate the full extent of God's grace, enabling us to respond to life's challenges with compassion and forgiveness. Through Jesus, we receive the strength to lead, serve, and love in ways that reflect God's heart for humanity.

Big Idea: Embrace shared leadership and wisdom in the community to reflect God's order and grace in every aspect of life.

Reflection: How are you sharing the burdens and responsibilities in your community? Are you seeking wisdom and guidance from others, and how might this open you up to deeper spiritual insights? Finally, in what ways can you embody Christ's servant leadership in your own life?

Prayer: Gracious God, guide us in wisdom and humility as we navigate our roles within your kingdom. Help us to bear each other's burdens with grace and to lead with a servant's heart, reflecting your love and justice in all we do. Strengthen us by your Spirit to live out the truths of Exodus 18, that we may be a light to those around us. In the name of Jesus, our example and enabler, we pray. Amen.

Day 25

Called to Holiness

Reading: Exodus 19

Exodus 19 marks a critical juncture in the journey of Israel, a moment where the divine meets the earthly amid thunder, lightning, and a thick cloud on Mount Sinai. This chapter isn't merely a historical account. It's a profound narrative about covenant, calling, and the nature of a holy God inviting a people to live in a special relationship.

This passage is a dramatic declaration of God's sovereignty and holiness. The mountain is more than geography; it symbolizes God's majestic and unapproachable holiness. Yet, amid this, there is an invitation—a call to be a "kingdom of priests and a holy nation." This isn't just ancient history but a narrative that speaks into the very fabric of our spiritual identity today.

For our spiritual lives, Exodus 19 serves as a reminder of our unique calling as believers. Just as Israel was called to be distinct and set apart, so are we invited into a life that mirrors God's holiness and love. This chapter challenges us to consider what it means to be a community centered on divine principles, living out a higher standard in a world that often settles for less.

The themes of Exodus 19 have profound implications for how we live as Christians. The holiness of God demands a response of reverence, obedience, and a commitment to justice and righteousness. It calls for a community that embodies reconciliation, humility, and service, reflecting the character of God in every interaction. In a world fractured by division and strife, the call to be a "kingdom of priests" is a call to bridge gaps, to be agents of peace, and to demonstrate a different way of living that echoes divine compassion and forgiveness.

Pointing to Jesus, Exodus 19 finds its ultimate fulfillment. Christ, the one who perfectly embodies God's holiness, invites us into a new covenant. We can approach the divine presence without fear through his life, death, and resurrection. In Jesus, we find the grace to live out our holy calling, empowered by the Spirit to walk in love, service, and obedience.

Big Idea: Live as a distinct and holy community, reflecting God's righteousness and grace in every aspect of life.

Reflection: How does your life reflect the holy calling to which you've been invited? How can you commit to justice, peace, and reconciliation daily?

Prayer: Holy God, who called Israel to be a holy nation, call us afresh to live out our divine purpose. Help us to understand the depth of your holiness and to respond with lives that reflect your love, justice, and righteousness. Empower us through your Spirit to be a community that lives in the reality of your grace, following the example of Jesus, our Savior and Lord. Amen.

Day 26

Pathways of Holiness

Reading: Exodus 20

Exodus 20, standing at the heart of the Sinai narrative, presents the Decalogue or the Ten Commandments. This isn't merely a list of rules but a covenantal framework guiding Israel's relationship with God and each other. These commandments are foundational, not just to Israel's society, but as eternal principles reflecting God's character and the blueprint for a just and moral society.

These commandments are more than ancient law; they reflect God's nature and a blueprint for human flourishing. They address our relationship with God and one another, covering the spectrum of morality, justice, and personal integrity. Each commandment unwraps a principle that, when lived out, leads to a life of harmony and peace with God and community.

For our spiritual lives, Exodus 20 is a mirror reflecting our need for divine guidance. It's a reminder of the holiness God desires, and the grace provided to live up to this high calling. These aren't just rules to follow but a path to walk, a journey towards a deeper, more meaningful relationship with the Divine and our community. They remind us that our actions, words, and thoughts matter deeply, shaping our lives and world.

Living out Exodus 20 today means embracing these principles as more than moral codes; they are the contours of a life lived in God's shadow. They call us to justice, urging us to stand against inequality and oppression. They beckon us to reconcile, mend broken relationships, and seek peace. They challenge us to love in words and deeds, show compassion, offer forgiveness, serve humbly, and live faithfully.

Jesus, the embodiment of the law, brings these commandments to their fullest expression. In him, the law is not abolished but fulfilled. His life, death, and resurrection provide the means to aspire to the holiness the commandments depict. He enables us to live out these divine principles through his grace working within us.

Big Idea: Embrace God's commandments as a path to live justly, love mercy, and walk humbly with God and others.

Reflection: How do the Ten Commandments reflect in your daily interactions and decisions? How can you embody these principles to reflect Christ's love and grace more fully?

Prayer: Sovereign Lord, who provided the Ten Commandments as a guide for holy living, engrave your laws on our hearts. Help us understand the depth of your holiness and love so that we might lead lives worthy of the calling you have placed upon us. The power of your Spirit and the example of Christ enable us to embody justice, reconciliation, and love. In Jesus's name, we pray. Amen.

Day 27

Justice and Mercy Intertwined

Reading: Exodus 21

Exodus 21 delves into the specifics of Israelite law, presenting a challenging text dealing with justice, servitude, and personal injury. While these ancient laws may seem distant, they provide profound insights into God's character and the societal norms God established for a just community. This chapter is part of a more extensive covenantal code, aiming to regulate social behavior and promote a society where the vulnerable are protected and justice is sought.

For our spiritual lives, Exodus 21 invites deep reflection on the nature of justice and how it is applied. It pushes us to consider our responsibility towards others, especially the marginalized and oppressed. The passage challenges us to see God's law not as a burden but as a framework designed to foster a community where dignity, respect, and fairness are upheld.

In living out the principles found in Exodus 21, Christians are called to be advocates for justice and peace. While culturally specific, the chapter underscores enduring principles like the sanctity of life, the importance of community, and the need for restitution and reconciliation when wrong is done. It encourages a posture of humility, service, and compassion, reminding us that our actions towards others reflect our reverence for God.

Jesus, in his life and teachings, embodies the perfect fulfillment of the law, including the principles laid out in Exodus 21. He teaches us to love our neighbors, to seek justice, and to offer forgiveness. We receive the grace needed to live out these challenging commands through him. He enables us to pursue justice, not through our strength but through the power of his transformative love.

Big Idea: Act justly, love mercy, and pursue reconciliation as reflections of God's righteous and compassionate character.

Reflection: How does your understanding of justice align with the principles outlined in this chapter? How can you actively participate in creating a community that reflects God's justice, compassion, and love?

Prayer: Gracious God, guide us in understanding your laws and living them out with integrity and compassion. Help us to see your justice as a reflection of your love and to be agents of reconciliation and peace in our communities. Strengthen us through your Spirit to love and serve those around us, following the example of Jesus, in whose name we pray. Amen.

Day 28

Living Justly, Loving Mercy

Reading: Exodus 22

Exodus 22 continues the covenantal code, detailing laws that guide the Israelites to live together justly and compassionately. These laws address various issues, from property restitution to social responsibility, each revealing an aspect of God's concern for order, justice, and mercy. These rules aren't arbitrary decrees but reflections of God's character and guidelines for creating a community where respect and fairness are paramount.

For our spiritual lives, Exodus 22 is a treasure trove of wisdom about living in harmony with others. It challenges us to consider how our actions impact our neighbors and pushes us to think beyond our interests. The passage calls us to a life marked by empathy, where we see the needs of the vulnerable and respond with compassion. It's about taking responsibility for our actions and their effects on the community and the world.

In terms of Christian living, Exodus 22 provides concrete examples of what it looks like to embody the values of the kingdom of God. It invites us to engage in acts of peace, justice, reconciliation, and love. This chapter encourages us to be people of integrity who care for our neighbors, forgive as we have been forgiven, and show mercy as a reflection of the mercy we've received. It's a call to be proactive in righting wrongs and to be generous, reflecting God's generosity to us.

Jesus, who said he came not to abolish the law but to fulfill it, embodies the principles of Exodus 22 perfectly. He is our model of compassion, justice, and love. Through his life and teachings, we learn the fullest expression of what it means to live out these laws. His sacrifice and resurrection enable us to live in this new way, empowering us by his Spirit to pursue righteousness, love, and peace.

Big Idea: Embrace and practice God's justice and mercy daily as a testament to God's loving character.

Reflection: How do the principles in this chapter shape your understanding of justice and compassion? How can you apply these laws to your life, showing others God's love and mercy?

Prayer: Eternal God, who provided guidelines for just and compassionate living in Exodus 22, instill a deep understanding of your justice and mercy in us. Help us to live out these principles daily, reflecting your love and care for all creation. Empower us by your Spirit to be agents of reconciliation and peace, following the example of Jesus, in whose name we pray. Amen.

Day 29

Divine Rhythms of Grace

Reading: Exodus 23:1-19

This passage lays a foundation for social ethics, emphasizing the importance of honesty, fairness, and protection of the vulnerable. These laws are more than societal guidelines; they are divine mandates calling us to a higher moral standard. The prohibition against spreading false rumors, the command to avoid false charges, and the instruction not to follow the crowd in doing wrong highlight a divine concern for truth, mercy, and justice. They urge us to look beyond our interests and consider the well-being and dignity of others.

The sabbatical laws in verses 10-12 move us from justice between humans to rest and renewal for the land and the laborer. These laws teach us about the rhythm of work and rest, not just for personal benefit but for the health of the entire creation. The command to rest every seventh year and every seventh day point to a Creator who cares for the land and the laborer. It's a reminder that our lives are not our own but intertwined with the rhythms of creation and the Creator's design.

In verses 13-19, the focus shifts to the proper worship of God, highlighting festivals and offerings. These instructions remind us that worship is not an isolated act but is connected to daily life and ethics. The festivals celebrate God's provision and deliverance, reinforcing the community's identity and purpose. They are not just religious rituals; they are communal practices that shape the people's understanding of God, justice, and mercy.

What does this ancient text mean for our spiritual lives today? It calls us to embody God's justice, mercy, and compassion in our everyday actions. It reminds us that our faith is not just a personal matter but is deeply connected to community, creation, and worship. It challenges us to be people of integrity, justice, and rest in a world that often promotes deceit, injustice, and constant labor.

As followers of Christ, we see in Jesus the perfect embodiment of these laws. He is the one who brought justice, offered rest, and lived out the perfect worship of the Father. His life and teachings guide us in responding to the themes of Exodus 23. Through his love and grace, we are empowered to pursue peace, seek reconciliation, act humbly, serve others, show compassion, and forgive. In doing so, we not only obey the letter of the law but also fulfill its spirit.

Big Idea: Live out God's justice, mercy, and rest to reflect Jesus's transformative love in every aspect of life.

Reflection: How can we more faithfully embody the justice and compassion of Exodus 23 in our community? How can we find rest and renewal for ourselves and creation?

Prayer: Sovereign Creator, guide us by your word and Spirit to live out the profound teachings of Exodus 23. Please help us to embody your justice, compassion, mercy, and rest in our lives. Strengthen us to serve you faithfully, reflecting the love and grace of Jesus in all we do. Amen.

Day 30

Guided by Grace

Reading: Exodus 23:20-33

In this passage, God promises guidance and protection through an angel, insisting on obedience and promising blessings of place and prosperity. It's a narrative woven with themes of guidance, faithfulness, and divine assurance.

At its core, this Scripture is about God's commitment to lead and protect. The angel is more than a heavenly being; it symbolizes God's presence. The command to obey the angel reflects a profound call to align with God's will, recognizing divine authority in our lives. These verses are a historical promise to Israel and a timeless call to understand divine guidance.

God tells Israel and us to trust divine guidance, worship the Lord our God, and reject idolatry and its practices. We know from other passages that God also commands us to bless the nations, the earth, and all creation, being a light of restoration, healing, peace, and blessing.

This passage is about the journey we're all on, the journey of faith. The promise of an angel to guard us is a metaphor for God's guidance through the Holy Spirit. We're called to listen, follow, and trust God's path. This isn't just about ancient Israel; it's about every one of us today. We're reminded that obedience isn't about legalistic rule-following but a relationship of trust and love with the Divine.

This journey with God isn't just personal; it has communal, societal implications. The text speaks of God driving out nations, which can be troubling. Yet, when we view this through a lens of spiritual conquest, it speaks to the battles against injustice, hatred, and oppression. Christians are called to be agents of righteousness, peace, justice, hope, and reconciliation. This isn't about physical battles but about fighting against the wrongs in our world through love, humility, service, and forgiveness. We're called to love our neighbors and enemies, reflecting God's love and grace. Our lives must reflect the values of the kingdom of God and point people to Jesus Christ, our Lord and Savior.

In Jesus, we see the ultimate guide and protector, who embodies God's presence and shows us the way of love and obedience. He exemplifies the perfect response to God's guidance, living a life of love, service, and sacrifice. In Jesus, we see the enabling grace to live out the themes of Exodus 23:20–33. The Spirit of Christ empowers us to walk in obedience, seek justice, love mercy, and walk humbly with our God.

Big Idea: Embrace God's guidance with obedience and love, actively seeking justice and peace as reflections of divine presence in the world.

Reflection: How are you experiencing God's guidance in your life? In what ways are you called to embody justice, peace, and love in your community? How does the example of Jesus inspire you to live out these themes in your daily life?

Prayer: Divine Guide, lead us on the path of righteousness. Help us hear your voice and see your hand at work in our lives. Empower us to live out your call to justice, love, and peace. May we walk in the footsteps of Jesus, embodying your love and grace to all. Amen.

Day 31

Covenant Commitment

Reading: Exodus 24

In Exodus 24, we find ourselves at the foot of Mount Sinai, witnessing a moment of profound commitment and divine covenant. The scene unfolds as the people of Israel affirm their pledge to follow God's commands, a solemn promise met with a spectacular sign of God's presence. This passage is not merely an ancient contract. It is a vibrant, living invitation to understand the depth of the divine-human relationship.

At the heart of this chapter is the theme of commitment. The Israelites affirm, "All the words which Yahweh has spoken we will do," a statement echoing through the ages to challenge us in our spiritual journey. This isn't about legalistic adherence but a heartfelt response to a loving God. The sprinkling of blood on the altar and the people signifies more than a ritual—it's a powerful symbol of life given and shared, pointing to a future where sacrifice and covenant find their fulfillment.

What, then, does Exodus 24 mean for our spiritual lives today? It's a call to remember that our faith is not a solitary endeavor but a communal journey. The shared meal of the elders on Mount Sinai reminds us of the Eucharist, where we, too, are invited to sit in God's presence and be nourished. Our response to God's word should be one of action and reflection, embodying the principles of justice, reconciliation, and love in our daily lives. The covenant at Sinai asks us to consider not just our vertical relationship with God but our horizontal relationships with others.

Exodus 24 challenges us to live out our faith with a commitment that mirrors Israel's promise. This means pursuing peace, enacting justice, and embodying compassion in a world rife with conflict and need. The text invites us to a life of humility and service, reflecting the character of God, who is revealed not in thunder and lightning but in a still, small voice. As we navigate our modern wildernesses, the principles of forgiveness and loving our neighbors and even our enemies become not just lofty ideals but concrete daily practices.

This ancient story points us to Jesus, who fulfills the covenant and invites us into a new relationship with God. Through him, we see the ultimate expression of love, enabling, and grace. His life, death, and resurrection embody the themes of Exodus 24, offering us a model of discipleship that goes beyond mere observance to a transformative way of living.

Big Idea: Pursue justice, peace, and love as a response to God's covenant invitation.

Reflection: How does my life reflect the commitment made by the Israelites at Sinai? In what ways am I being called to embody justice, peace, and love in my community?

Prayer: Divine Presence, who met your people at Sinai, meet us in our daily journeys. Infuse our actions with your love and grace so we might live out the covenant you have written on our hearts. Help us to love, serve, and forgive as we have been loved, served, and forgiven. In the name of the One who fulfills all promises, amen.

Day 32

Divine Dwelling Within

Reading: Exodus 25

Exodus 25 sketches the blueprint for the tabernacle. This isn't merely an architectural project; it's a divine call for creating a sacred space where heaven and earth overlap. This space symbolizes God's desire to dwell among us, offering an intimate relationship despite our imperfections.

Consider the detailed instructions for the ark of the covenant, the table for bread, and the golden lampstand. Each element is rich in symbolism, reflecting aspects of God's nature and ways. With its mercy seat, the ark represents God's throne, hinting at divine justice tempered with mercy. The table with bread signifies God's provision, reminding us of our daily dependence on the divine. With its perpetually burning lights, the lampstand symbolizes God's guiding presence.

What does this ancient text mean for our spiritual lives today? It speaks of a God who doesn't remain distant but desires to dwell within us. Our hearts become the tabernacle, the sacred space where God resides. This indwelling prompts a transformation where our lives reflect divine attributes—justice, mercy, provision, and guidance.

As we embody these attributes, our lives naturally align with themes of mercy, worship, holiness, justice, and divine provision. The tabernacle was a communal project requiring diverse gifts and united effort. Similarly, we're called to build communities grounded in love, humility, and service. This isn't a passive existence but an active participation in God's redemptive work, worshipping God in holiness, trusting God's guidance and provision, seeking justice for the oppressed, offering forgiveness as we've forgiven, and loving our neighbors and enemies and those who've arrived in our context from other cultures, religions, and lands.

Furthermore, Exodus 25 points us to Jesus. In the New Testament, John writes of Jesus, "The Word became flesh and lived among us" (John 1:14). Jesus is the true tabernacle, the perfect meeting place between God and humanity. His life, death, and resurrection embody the ultimate expression of divine love, justice, and mercy. Through Jesus, we receive the grace to respond to God's call, empowered to reflect divine love in a broken world.

Big Idea: Embrace your life as a living tabernacle, reflecting God's love and justice in your Christian and local community.

Reflection: How does the image of God desiring to dwell within you change your understanding of your daily life? In what ways can you participate in creating a community that reflects divine attributes of justice, mercy, and love?

Prayer: Divine Architect, who sketched the tabernacle and the cosmos blueprint, guide us in crafting lives that reflect your beauty and truth. Help us to understand the depth of your desire to dwell within us and empower us to live as bearers of your light, mercy, righteousness, justice, and love. May our lives be sacred spaces where others can encounter your grace. Amen.

Day 33

Sanctuary of the Spirit

Reading: Exodus 26

In Exodus 26, we find a meticulous description of the tabernacle, a sacred dwelling for the Divine. More than a simple list of instructions, this detailed narrative invites us to a profound understanding of God's desire to dwell among God's people. The materials—acacia wood, fine linen, and precious metals—reflect the value and beauty of this divine-human meeting place. But beyond the physical structure, Exodus 26 speaks to deeper spiritual truths.

This passage is a vibrant tapestry of symbolism. Each element, from the curtains to the clasps, signifies our interconnectedness with the Divine. With its innermost sanctum, the tabernacle represents the heart, where God wishes to reside. The layers of curtains, dyed with heavenly blue and royal purple, illustrate the layers of our soul, woven together, designed to be a dwelling place for God. The resilient and enduring acacia wood mirrors the steadfastness we're called to embody.

Exodus 26 is not merely an ancient construction manual but a blueprint for our spiritual lives. It urges us to build our lives as a sanctuary for the Divine, inviting us to consider what materials we use. Are they of enduring quality, reflective of beauty and truth? This passage beckons us to consider the structure of our "tabernacles"—how we create space for the Divine in our hearts and communities. Just as the tabernacle was the center of Israel's camp, we are called to make God's presence the center of our lives.

Living out the themes of Exodus 26 means crafting our lives into sanctuaries of peace, justice, and reconciliation. It's about cultivating humility, service, and compassion as the "curtains" and "clasps" that hold our spiritual dwellings together. We're called to weave our lives with threads of forgiveness and love, extending the sanctuary beyond ourselves to our neighbors and even our enemies.

This divine blueprint also points us to Jesus, the ultimate meeting place between the Divine and humanity. In Christ, we see the perfect tabernacle, the Word made flesh, dwelling among us. His life exemplifies the beauty and intricacy of a life wholly dedicated to God. Through Jesus, we're enabled to respond to the call of Exodus 26, to construct our lives as places where God's presence is felt and known.

Big Idea: Build your life as a sanctuary where God's presence dwells and radiates love and reconciliation.

Reflection: What materials are you using to build your spiritual life? How does your life reflect the beauty and holiness of a dwelling place for God? Finally, how might you extend the borders of your sanctuary to include others, especially those in need of love and reconciliation?

Prayer: Divine Architect, guide us as we build our lives into sanctuaries for you. Please help us choose materials that reflect your beauty and truth. May our hearts be places where your presence is felt and known. Strengthen us by your grace to extend the borders of our sanctuary, to love, serve, and reconcile as Jesus did. Amen.

Day 34

Living Altars

Reading: Exodus 27

Exodus 27, with its detailed instructions for the altar of burnt offerings and the tabernacle courtyard, invites us to a deeper understanding of God's desire for a space where divine and human spheres meet. This chapter isn't just about constructing a physical space.It's about preparing our hearts to be a place of continuous offering and encounter with the Divine.

The bronze altar, central to the chapter, symbolizes a place of sacrifice and atonement. It's a vivid picture of transformation, where what is offered is changed, consumed by holy fire. This isn't merely an ancient ritual but a profound metaphor for our spiritual lives. We're called to offer ourselves daily, let our lives be transformed by God's holy fire, and become a living sacrifice characterized by love, humility, and service.

The courtyard described in Exodus 27 represents boundaries that define sacred space. These boundaries are healthy spiritual disciplines and moral principles that help us maintain a holy space in our hearts for God. Just as the Israelites were to keep the lamp burning continually, we're called to nurture a continuous flame of faith and devotion. This isn't a call to occasional spirituality but to a constant, abiding relationship with the Divine.

How, then, do we live out the lessons of Exodus 27? By cultivating a life of continuous offering and sacred space. It means seeking justice, loving mercy, and walking humbly with God. It's about serving others in grand gestures and everyday acts of kindness and compassion. It's about forgiveness, not as a one-time act but as a continual posture of the heart. It's about embodying the peace and reconciliation we've received, extending it to neighbors and enemies alike.

Jesus embodies the ultimate altar and courtyard. We see the perfect sacrifice and the holy space where God and humanity meet in him. Through his life, death, and resurrection, Jesus enables us to become living sanctuaries, reflecting his light and love. Jesus invites us to join him in transforming the world, one act of love and service at a time.

Big Idea: Cultivate a life of continuous offering and sacred space, transforming daily with God's holy fire.

Reflection: As you reflect on Exodus 27, consider what needs to be offered and transformed in your life? How are you maintaining sacred space in your heart for God? How does your life reflect the continuous flame of faith and devotion?

Prayer: Eternal Flame, ignite our hearts with your divine fire. Help us offer every part of our lives to you for transformation. Guide us in maintaining a sacred space for you in our hearts. Empower us to live as continuous flames of faith, reflecting your love and light to the world. In the name of Jesus, our altar and courtyard. Amen.

Day 35

Garments of Grace

Reading: Exodus 28

Exodus 28 is a rich tapestry of spiritual symbolism, detailing the priestly garments designed for dignity and honor. This isn't just an ancient fashion statement. It's a profound narrative about identity, calling, and the beauty of serving before God. Each thread and gem reflects a deep spiritual truth about our role in the divine story.

The ephod, breastplate, and other garments the high priest wears are rich in symbolism. They signify carrying the people's names before God, representing their identity and burdens. The precious stones and fine materials represent God's value in this mediating role. This chapter is not merely about vestments but the calling to bear one another's burdens and intercede with compassion and dignity.

Exodus 28, therefore, speaks to our spiritual lives by inviting us to consider our priestly role. We, too, are called to bear the names and burdens of others before God in prayer and action. Like the priest's garments, our lives are to be woven with threads of love, justice, and righteousness. We're called to reflect God's beauty and holiness, standing in the gap for those around us, mediating not with our righteousness but clothed in the grace and love of Christ.

Living out the themes of Exodus 28 means embracing our calling as a royal priesthood, as Peter would later describe. It's about serving with humility, clothed in compassion and integrity. It's about seeking reconciliation in grand gestures and the quiet, often unseen work of intercession and peacemaking. It's about embodying justice and love, not as abstract concepts but as daily, tangible acts of service.

Jesus is the ultimate high priest, and in him, the intricate details of Exodus 28 find their fulfillment. He bore our names and burdens to the cross, interceding on our behalf. Through Jesus's sacrifice, he invites us into this priestly calling, enabling us by his grace to serve and love as he did. Christ Jesus clothes us with garments of salvation and robes of righteousness, empowering us to reflect his love and light to the world.

Big Idea: Embrace your priestly calling by bearing others' burdens with grace and reflecting Christ's love and holiness.

Reflection: How are you bearing the names and burdens of others before God? In what ways does your life reflect the beauty and holiness of Christ? How are you living out your calling as part of a royal priesthood?

Prayer: Gracious Intercessor, clothe us with your righteousness and grace. Help us to bear the burdens of others with dignity and love, reflecting your beauty and holiness in our lives. Empower us to live out our priestly calling, serving and interceding in your name. In the name of Jesus, our high priest and Redeemer. Amen.

Day 36

Sacred Reflections

Reading: Exodus 29

Exodus 29 presents the consecration of priests, a vivid and detailed account of how Aaron and his sons were set apart for God's service. This isn't merely an ancient ritual but a profound narrative about sanctification, sacrifice, and the presence of God among us. As we delve into its rich symbolism, we understand that it's more than instructions for a ceremony. It's a divine invitation to consider our consecration in the spiritual journey.

The rites of washing, clothing, anointing, and offering described in this chapter symbolize purification, dedication, and atonement. They're reminders of the need for inner and outer transformation to serve in God's presence. Just as Aaron and his sons were consecrated for a holy task, we too are called to be set apart, cleansed by God's grace, clothed in Christ's righteousness, and anointed by the Spirit for our divine purpose.

Exodus 29 speaks profoundly to our spiritual lives, emphasizing the significance of consecration for God's service. It invites us to consider what it means to be set apart, not in a way that isolates us from the world but through equipping us to serve with love, humility, and compassion. It's about recognizing our daily lives as an offering pleasing to God, and living in a way that reflects our sacred calling.

Living out the themes of Exodus 29 means embracing a life of continuous consecration and renewal. It's about seeking peace and justice, not as distant ideals but as realities we're called to embody. It's about reconciliation, recognizing that our consecration involves reconciling with others and helping mend broken relationships. It's about serving humbly, not considering ourselves above the least of these but as servants to all.

Jesus, our great high priest, is the ultimate fulfillment of Exodus 29. In him, we see the perfect sacrifice and consecration. Jesus enables us to live out our consecration through his life, death, and resurrection. He invites us into a life of sacrificial love, a life that mirrors his own, a life poured out for others.

Big Idea: Embrace continuous consecration, living as a reflection of Christ's sacrificial love and service.

Reflection: In what ways are you living out your consecration to God? How does your life reflect the sacrificial love and service that Jesus exemplified? How are you engaging in acts of peace, justice, and reconciliation as part of your sacred calling?

Prayer: Holy Consecrator, wash us anew with your grace, clothe us with your righteousness, and anoint us with your Spirit. Help us to live as consecrated servants, reflecting your love and light in every aspect of our lives. Empower us to embody peace, justice, and reconciliation, following the example of Jesus, our great high priest. Amen.

Day 37

Fragrance of Faith

Reading: Exodus 30

Exodus 30 details the intricate design of the tabernacle, focusing on the altar of incense, the census tax, and the anointing oil and incense. These aren't just architectural blueprints or ancient tax regulations but profound symbols of intercession, community, and holiness. Through them, we glimpse the depth of God's desire for a people set apart, continually seeking divine presence.

The altar of incense represents continual intercession, a perpetual offering of prayers rising to God. It's a powerful image of how our prayers, like sweet-smelling incense, should ascend continually before God. This teaches us the importance of persistent prayer and constant communion with the Divine. Much like the altar, our lives are to be places where the fragrance of intercession never ceases.

The census tax speaks to the value of everyone within the community of faith. Each person's contribution, a half shekel, was the same regardless of wealth, indicating that every person holds equal value and responsibility in the community. This reflects a profound spiritual truth about our equal standing before God and our shared call to contribute to God's kingdom work.

The anointing oil and incense symbolize sanctification and purity. Being set apart for God's service isn't just a matter of external rituals; it's about internal transformation. The unique blend of spices and oil wasn't to be replicated for common use, reminding us that the call to holiness is a distinct and sacred calling, not to be taken lightly or mingled with worldly patterns.

Exodus 30, therefore, informs how we should live as Christians. It calls us to a life of continual prayer and intercession, seeing our prayers as a sweet fragrance before God. It reminds us of our equal and valuable role within the community of faith, encouraging us to contribute and serve with humility and love. And it invites us to live a distinct holiness, set apart for God's purposes.

In his life and ministry, Jesus embodies the ultimate intercessor, community builder, and the Holy One set apart by God. Through him, we can live out the spiritual lessons of Exodus 30. Jesus's sacrifice makes our prayers acceptable, his teachings build a new community, and his Spirit anoints us for holy living.

Big Idea: Live as a continuous offering of prayer, equal service, and distinct holiness, reflecting Christ's intercession and love.

Reflection: How does your prayer life reflect the continual offering of incense before God? How are you contributing to and building up the community of faith? How are you pursuing a distinct life of holiness, set apart for God's service?

Prayer: Divine Intercessor, may our prayers rise before you like incense, a continual offering of our hearts. Please help us recognize and fulfill our role in your community, valuing everyone equally. Anoint us afresh, setting us apart for your holy purposes. In all we do, may we reflect the love and grace of Jesus. Amen.

Day 38

Crafted for Worship

Reading: Exodus 31

Exodus 31 unveils God's appointment of Bezalel and Oholiab, imbuing them with the Spirit, wisdom, understanding, and skill for constructing the tabernacle. This isn't merely a delegation of tasks; it's a divine endorsement of creativity and craftsmanship as acts of worship. The Sabbath is also reiterated here, not a burdensome command but a covenantal sign, a rhythm of work and rest.

This chapter beautifully illustrates that creativity and skill are divine gifts. Bezalel and Oholiab's calling dignifies every form of work and is a powerful reminder that all vocations can glorify God when done with excellence and a spirit-led heart. Their work on the tabernacle was an act of worship, integrating their skills with their faith. Likewise, our daily work, whatever it may be, is an opportunity to worship and serve God.

Exodus 31 also speaks profoundly to the rhythm of the Sabbath. It's a divine command to rest, to cease labor, and to reflect on God's provision and goodness. The Sabbath isn't merely a day off, it's a sacred time to reconnect with God and remember that our identity isn't based on what we do but on whom we belong to. It's a gift, offering us a regular reminder of grace and a rhythm that counters the ceaseless pace of life.

Living out the themes of Exodus 31 means recognizing and utilizing our God-given talents for his glory. It's about seeing our work as integral to our spiritual lives, not separate or secular. It's about embracing the Sabbath rest, understanding that it's not only a command but also a blessing that rejuvenates us and honors God. In doing so, we witness a different way of living, one that values diligent work and intentional rest.

Jesus, in his life and teachings, embodies the true Spirit of the Sabbath. He is the Lord of the Sabbath, inviting us into rest and relationship with him. Through Christ's life, death, and resurrection, he grants us rest from striving, enabling us by his grace to live in a rhythm of work, worship, service, and Sabbath.

Big Idea: Embrace your God-given talents and the sacred rhythm of the Sabbath as acts of worship and rest in Christ.

Reflection: How are you using your God-given talents to serve and glorify God? Are you incorporating a rhythm of Sabbath into your life, and what does that look like for you?

Prayer: Creator and Sustainer, thank you for the gifts and talents you've bestowed upon us. Help us use them to glorify you and serve others. Teach us the sacred rhythm of the Sabbath, to rest in your grace and provision. May our lives reflect the work and rest balance you desire, following the example of Jesus, our ultimate Rest and Redeemer. Amen.

Day 39

Grace Beyond Idols

Reading: Exodus 32

Exodus 32 is a poignant narrative, unfolding a drama of faith, idolatry, and divine mercy. At its core, this chapter confronts us with Israel's profound failure at the foot of Sinai. As Moses communes with God on the mountain, receiving the tablets of the covenant, the people, in their impatience and fear, craft a golden calf to worship.

This account is a historical recounting and a mirror reflecting our spiritual journey. The Israelites' turn to the golden calf echoes the human propensity to replace the divine with tangible, controllable substitutes. Their impatience and lack of trust are not ancient flaws but perennial human traits. This narrative beckons us to examine our hearts, to recognize the "golden calves" we may unknowingly worship—whether they be power, comfort, or control.

Yet, Exodus 32 is not a story of despair but a revelation of divine mercy and intercession. Moses, the mediator, stands in the breach, pleading for the people. This intercession points us to the ultimate Mediator, Jesus Christ, whose love and sacrifice bridge the chasm of our sin and rebellion. Just as Moses descended the mountain to restore the covenant, Christ descended from heaven to establish a new covenant, not on tablets of stone but human hearts.

The incident at Sinai challenges us to live as a people set apart. In a world marred by injustice, conflict, and self-centeredness, we are called to embody divine attributes—peace, justice, reconciliation, and compassion. As the Israelites were instructed to remove their ornaments as a sign of repentance, we too are called to lay aside every encumbrance, the sin that so easily entangles, and to walk humbly with our God.

We are reminded that our faith journey is not a solitary endeavor but a communal pursuit. Just as Israel was called to be a light to the nations, we are called to love our neighbors, seek the welfare of our communities, and be agents of reconciliation in a fractured world. This call is not born out of our strength but is a response to the unfathomable love and grace bestowed upon us through Christ.

Big Idea: Embrace Christ's enabling grace to identify and forsake our "golden calves," embodying his love and justice daily.

Reflection: What "golden calves" might you unwittingly worship? How does this narrative challenge you to live out peace, justice, and compassion daily? How does Christ's intercession and love empower you to respond to these themes?

Prayer: Gracious and Merciful God, who rescues us from our idolatries, instill in us a heart of faith that clings to you alone. Help us to discern the "golden calves" in our lives and grant us the courage to lay them down. Empower us by your Spirit to embody your love, justice, and peace in a world that desperately needs it. May our lives reflect the grace and truth of Christ, our Mediator and Redeemer. Amen.

Day 40

Presence Over Promise

Reading: Exodus 33

Exodus 33 is a chapter of profound intimacy and pivotal choices. We encounter a God imminently near and majestically transcendent as we traverse this sacred text. Following the golden calf debacle, we see a people stripped of their ornaments—a symbol of their stripped status before God. Yet, in this place of bareness, we witness the beauty of divine grace.

This chapter presents a compelling picture: Moses speaking to God "face to face, as one speaks to a friend." This is a historical event and a vibrant paradigm for our spiritual journey. We're invited into a relationship where honest conversation, heartfelt pleas, and divine responses are the norm. Here, in the tent of meeting, we find the heart of Christian spirituality—an authentic, ongoing dialogue with the Divine.

Exodus 33 also confronts us with a choice—to go with or without God. The pivotal moment comes when God promises to send an angel to lead the people into the promised land, but Moses insists, "If your presence doesn't go with me, don't carry us up from here" (v. 15). This is a profound recognition that the greatest blessing is not the land itself but the presence of God within it.

This narrative challenges us to consider what we are pursuing in our lives. Are we content with God's blessings or seek God's presence? In our endeavors for peace, justice, and reconciliation, are we driven by the desire to make a name for ourselves, or are we motivated by a deep longing to walk in step with the Divine?

As Christians, we are called to reflect the nature of God in the world. This means embodying love, humility, service, faith, and compassion. These are ethical duties, and the natural outflow of a life lived in God's presence. When we abide in the Divine, we cannot help but spill over with divine love and grace to those around us, including our enemies and neighbors.

Moreover, Exodus 33 points us to Jesus, the one in whom we see the glory of God most clearly revealed. Just as Moses longed to see God's glory, we look to Christ, the "image of the invisible God." In him, we find the enabling grace to live out this chapter's themes, walk in intimate fellowship with God, and reflect divine love in our broken world.

Big Idea: Seek God's presence above all else, for in walking intimately with the Divine, we embody his love and transform the world.

Reflection: In what areas of your life are you seeking God's blessings more than God's presence? How might a deeper awareness of God's nearness transform your approach to the challenges and relationships in your life?

Prayer: Divine Presence, draw us more deeply into the holy ground of your companionship. May we seek your face more than your hand and in doing so become bearers of your love, justice, and peace to a world in need. Empower us by your Spirit to reflect the glory of Christ in every word we speak and every action we take. Amen.

Day 41

Renewed Covenant, Transformed Lives

Reading: Exodus 34:1-28

Exodus 34:1-28 is a testament to God's relentless grace and covenantal faithfulness. As we delve into this passage, we witness the Divine reestablishing a broken covenant, revealing the Divine nature, and outlining the way of life for the covenant community. This is not merely an ancient ritual but a vivid depiction of restoration and hope.

In this chapter, Moses ascends Sinai once more, but this time he carries two new tablets, symbolizing restoration and second chances. God proclaims the Divine nature: compassionate, gracious, slow to anger, abounding in love and faithfulness. These are not just attributes but an invitation to know the Divine more deeply, to be transformed by this character, and to reflect these qualities in our lives.

Exodus 34:1-28 invites us to consider the nature of divine forgiveness and the response it requires. The covenant renewal is a divine decree and a call to a transformed life. God's steadfast love and faithfulness demand a response of obedience, a commitment to a way of life that reflects the Divine character.

For our spiritual lives, this passage mirrors our need for continual renewal. Just as Moses returned up the mountain, we are called to return to God for fresh encounters and new beginnings. The renewal of the covenant reminds us that our relationship with the Divine is not static but dynamic, not a one-time event but an ongoing journey of transformation.

This journey is marked by a call to embody the Divine attributes in our interactions and society. Justice, reconciliation, love, humility, and compassion are not optional extras, but the very fabric of a life lived in covenant with God. As followers of Christ, we are called to be a community that reflects God's compassion and faithfulness and embodies divine love in action.

Exodus 34:1–28 also points us to Jesus, who embodies God's compassionate and gracious character perfectly. In Christ, we see the ultimate expression of divine love and the fulfillment of the covenant. Through his life, death, and resurrection, we are offered grace upon grace, enabling us to respond to God's faithfulness with discipleship and obedience.

Big Idea: Continually return to God for renewal, embodying divine compassion and faithfulness in every aspect of life.

Reflection: In what areas of your life do you need a new beginning with God? How might a deeper understanding of God's compassionate and gracious nature transform how you live and relate to others?

Prayer: Gracious and Compassionate God, who renews the covenant and restores the broken, engrave your character on our hearts. Renew us daily in your grace and empower us to live as a reflection of your love and faithfulness. May our lives be a testament to your transformative power and an embodiment of your justice, peace, and compassion. Amen.

Day 42

Radiant Reflections

Reading: Exodus 34:29-35

Exodus 34:29-35 narrates the radiant transformation of Moses after encountering the Divine on Mount Sinai. As Moses descends, his face is aglow with the reflected glory of God, so much so that he must veil his face among the people. This vivid image is a powerful metaphor for the transformative encounter with the Divine presence.

This passage symbolically illustrates the profound change that occurs within us when we spend time in God's presence. Moses' radiant face is a testament to the fact that close communion with the Divine alters us, influencing our inward disposition and outward demeanor. It's a compelling reminder that spiritual formation is not merely about internal change but a transformation visible to those around us.

In our spiritual lives, Exodus 34:29-35 invites us to consider the nature of our encounters with God. Are they transforming us in a way that is noticeable to others? Just as Moses' face shone, our lives should reflect the character and love of God to those we interact with daily. The "veil" Moses wore can symbolize the barriers we put up, preventing others from seeing God's work in our lives. We are called to remove these veils, allowing the divine light within us to shine.

For Christians, this radiant transformation should inform how we live. It's not enough to experience God's presence. We must reflect it in acts of peace, justice, reconciliation, love, humility, and compassion. These are moral imperatives and the natural outflow of a life lit up by the divine. As we bask in God's presence, we become agents of God's love in a world that often dwells in spiritual darkness.

Moreover, this passage points us to Jesus, who is described in the New Testament as the ultimate revelation of God's glory. In Christ, we see the full radiance of God's love and grace; through him, we are offered the chance to be transformed from one degree of glory to another. This transformation is not by our power but through the enabling grace of Christ, who works within us.

Big Idea: Let God's presence transform you visibly, so your life reflects Divine love and grace to the world radiantly.

Reflection: How is your time with God reflected in your daily interactions? What "veils" might you remove to let God's transformative light shine through you more clearly?

Prayer: God of Unveiled Glory, illuminate our hearts with your presence. Transform us into your image and help us to reflect your love and grace in every aspect of our lives. May our encounters with you be evident, drawing others into your radiant light. Through the grace of Jesus Christ, enable us to be faithful bearers of your glory. Amen.

Day 43

United in God's Work

Reading: Exodus 35

Exodus 35 unfolds a powerful narrative of community, generosity, and collaboration in constructing the tabernacle. This chapter is not merely an ancient account of building a dwelling place for God but a poignant metaphor for the spiritual life and faith community.

At the heart of Exodus 35 is the call to willing and generous contributions toward the construction of the tabernacle. This isn't a tax or levy. It's an invitation to participate in something divine. The materials are diverse, from gold and silver to yarn and goat hair, representing the varied gifts and resources each person brings. This is a profound picture of the church: diverse individuals coming together, offering what they have to create a dwelling place for God's presence.

For our spiritual lives, Exodus 35 is a reminder of the joy and privilege of contributing to God's work. Our offerings, whether time, talents, or treasure, are not burdens but blessings. They are part of how we engage with God and with each other in the sacred task of building up the community of faith and extending God's kingdom.

Moreover, Exodus 35 calls us to a spirit of collaboration and humility. The tabernacle was not built by a few skilled artisans but by the entire community, each person doing their part. Similarly, the church is built up not by a few but by many, each using their gifts to serve others. This requires a humble recognition of our need for each other and a willingness to work together for a common purpose.

This passage also speaks to the importance of rest and worship. Before the work begins, the Israelites are reminded to observe the Sabbath. This is not a pause in the work but an integral part. It's a reminder that our work is not the ultimate goal but that our ultimate rest and worship are found in God. In our busy lives, we also need this reminder to rest, worship, and see our ultimate purpose in God, not our work.

Exodus 35 points us to Jesus, the one in whom we see the ultimate expression of generosity and service. In Christ, we find the grace to give generously, serve humbly, and work together to build the church. His life, death, and resurrection enable us to be part of this divine building project, creating a community where God's presence dwells.

Big Idea: Embrace generous collaboration in God's work, building a community where his presence dwells through our diverse gifts.

Reflection: What gifts and resources can you offer to the work of God in your community? How can you collaborate more effectively with others in this sacred task?

Prayer: Generous God, who invites us to participate in your divine work, instill a spirit of generosity and collaboration in us. Help us to offer our gifts willingly, to serve humbly, and to work together for the building up of your church. May our lives reflect the love and grace of Jesus, in whose name we pray. Amen.

Day 44

Crafting the Kingdom

Reading: Exodus 36

Exodus 36 unfolds with the community of Israel coming together, each person contributing what they have to the construction of the tabernacle—God's dwelling place among them. This chapter isn't merely about the physical construction of a sanctuary but also a profound illustration of God's people uniting in a shared mission, reflecting the Divine image through creativity, generosity, and craftsmanship.

This narrative resonates deeply with our spiritual lives. It reminds us that we, as the church, are called to represent God's presence in the world collectively. Just as the Israelites brought their offerings for the tabernacle, we are invited to bring our gifts, talents, and resources to build up the body of Christ. Our contributions, no matter how small or insignificant they might seem, are valuable and essential in God's economy.

Exodus 36 speaks to the heart of Christian living. It's a call to active participation in God's work, not as isolated individuals but as a committed community. The artisans Bezalel and Oholiab, endowed with wisdom by God, guide the people in their work. This is a beautiful picture of how God equips and empowers us to contribute to his kingdom. It's a reminder that our faith isn't just a private affair but a communal endeavor, where each person's work, guided by divine wisdom, contributes to the greater whole.

Moreover, this chapter emphasizes the principle of generosity. The people bring more than enough materials for the tabernacle, demonstrating a heart of overflowing generosity. This isn't just about material giving but about a spirit of abundance that trusts in God's provision and looks beyond personal needs to the community's needs.

Exodus 36 also points us to Jesus, the one in whom the fullness of God was pleased to dwell. In Christ, we see the perfect embodiment of wisdom, generosity, and craftsmanship—the one who crafted salvation with the wood of the cross and the nails of suffering. Through him, we are invited into this divine project, building not just a physical sanctuary but a living one of people from every tribe, tongue, and nation.

Big Idea: Contribute wholeheartedly to God's work, trusting in his provision and uniting purposefully to reflect his presence in the world.

Reflection: How are you contributing to building God's kingdom in your community? How can you cultivate a spirit of generosity and trust in God's abundant provision?

Prayer: Creator God, who skillfully designed the universe, help us to see our part in your divine project. Fill us with wisdom and generosity so that we might contribute to the building up of your kingdom. May our lives reflect the love and grace of Jesus, in whose name we offer our gifts and ourselves. Amen.

Day 45

Sacred Craft

Reading: Exodus 37

Exodus 37 details the meticulous craftsmanship of the tabernacle's furnishings, from the ark of the covenant to the lampstand. Each piece, wrought by the skilled hands of Bezalel and other artisans, was a functional item and a rich symbol of God's presence and promises. This chapter isn't just an ancient inventory; it's a profound narrative of devotion, skill, and the sacredness imbued in everyday work.

Exodus 37 offers a powerful reminder for our spiritual lives that no work is too mundane or ordinary when done in service to God. The care and precision that Bezalel applied to craft the tabernacle furnishings mirror the attention we are called to give to our daily tasks. Whether crafting a piece of furniture, writing a report, or engaging in conversation, we are called to do it all for the glory of God.

This passage also speaks to the importance of using God-given talents to serve the community. Just as Bezalel and the artisans were endowed with skill, wisdom, and understanding, so are we equipped with various gifts. Our calling is not to hide these talents but to use them to build up Christ's body and bring beauty and order to our world.

Exodus 37 also invites us to reflect on the sacredness of space and how our environment can draw us closer to God. Just as the ark and the lampstand were central to the tabernacle worship, we must create spaces that remind us of God's presence and invite us into worship. Whether it's a corner of a room for prayer or a routine that centers us on God, creating sacred space is vital for our spiritual journey.

Moreover, this chapter points us to Jesus, the one in whom the fullness of God's presence dwelt. In Jesus Christ, we see the ultimate artisan, whose life, death, and resurrection crafted a way for us to enter God's presence. Through him, we are invited to become artisans in our own right, building a kingdom where love, justice, peace, and reconciliation are the cornerstones.

Big Idea: Dedicate your talents and tasks to God's glory, crafting your life as a testament to his enduring presence and love.

Reflection: How can you apply Bezalel's devotion and skill to your daily tasks? What gifts has God given you, and how can you use them for his glory?

Prayer: Creator God, who fashioned the universe with care and precision, imbue our work with your spirit of excellence and devotion. Please help us use our talents for your glory, create beauty and order in our world, and craft spaces that draw us and others closer to you. May our lives reflect the love and grace of Jesus, in whose name we build and serve. Amen.

Day 46

Sacred Communion

Reading: Exodus 38

Exodus 38 continues the detailed account of constructing the tabernacle, focusing on the altar of burnt offerings, the basin for washing, and the courtyard. These elements are not merely functional but deeply symbolic, representing sacrifice, purification and delineating a sacred space where God and humanity meet. While rich in ancient liturgical detail, this chapter carries profound implications for our spiritual lives today.

The altar of burnt offering speaks to the necessity of sacrifice in our approach to God. In our modern context, this doesn't imply animal sacrifices but offering our lives, wills, and desires to God. It's a daily practice of laying down our ego, plans, and comforts at the altar of God's greater purposes. This is not a loss but a liberation, freeing us from the burden of self to embrace the freedom found in divine surrender.

The basin for washing symbolizes the need for continual purification. Just as the priests needed to be cleansed before serving in the tabernacle, we, too, need regular spiritual renewal. This cleansing isn't a one-time event but an ongoing process of confession, forgiveness, and transformation. It's a reminder that we are continually being made new, washed by the water of the word and the Spirit.

The construction of the courtyard delineates a sacred space, setting apart the holy from the common. This speaks to the need to create spaces and rhythms that remind us of God's presence and draw us into deeper communion with the Divine. Whether it's a place in our homes for prayer or a time set aside for reflection, these sacred spaces are vital for our spiritual health and growth.

Exodus 38 also points us to Jesus, who fulfilled the symbolism of the altar and the basin. In Jesus Christ, the ultimate sacrifice was made, and through his life, death, and resurrection, we are offered the ultimate purification. His love, enabling, and grace empowers us to live sacrificially, embrace continual renewal, and cultivate sacred spaces in our lives and communities.

Big Idea: Embrace sacrifice, purification, and sacred space to deepen your communion with God and embody his presence to others.

Reflection: What must you lay on the altar today? How can you incorporate spiritual cleansing and renewal into your daily routine? What sacred spaces can you create or seek to deepen your relationship with God?

Prayer: Eternal God, who provided a way for your people to draw near, help us to lay our lives on your altar, seek your cleansing, and create sacred spaces where we can meet with you. May our lives reflect the sacrifice and purification found in Jesus, and may we be a living tabernacle of your presence to those around us. Amen.

Day 47

Clothed in Holiness

Reading: Exodus 39:1–31

Exodus 39:1–31 details the crafting of the priestly garments, designed with exquisite detail and profound symbolism. Each thread, stone, and weave is imbued with meaning, reflecting the priesthood's beauty, holiness, and mediating role. This passage is not just an ancient dress code but a a rich tapestry that speaks to the dignity and purpose with which God endows roles within the community.

The ephod, breast piece, and other garments were crafted to set the priests apart in their service to God. They were a visual reminder of their unique role as mediators between the Divine and the people. For our spiritual lives, this speaks to the idea that each of us, in our own way, is called to be a mediator of God's presence. As followers of Christ, we are a "royal priesthood" called to intercede, serve, and reflect God's character in the world.

The beauty and intricacy of the priestly garments also remind us that our service to God is not to be drab or perfunctory but filled with beauty, creativity, and care. Just as the garments were crafted with the finest materials and skill, so should our lives reflect a quality of devotion and excellence in all we do.

Exodus 39:1–31 also speaks to identity. The names of the tribes of Israel were engraved on stones and set on the ephod and breast piece, symbolizing the priest's representation of the people before God. This reminds us that we carry our community's concerns, pains, and joys. We are not isolated individuals but deeply connected to a broader body—our actions and prayers have a communal dimension.

Moreover, this passage points us to Jesus, our great high priest, who mediated God's presence and embodied it. In Jesus Christ, the fullness of God was pleased to dwell, and through his life, death, and resurrection, he opened a new and living way for us to approach the throne of grace. His sacrificial love and grace enable us to live out our priestly calling, serving and representing others before God.

Big Idea: Embrace your role as a mediator of God's presence, serving with beauty, devotion, and intercessory love.

Reflection: How does your life reflect the beauty and holiness of the service to which you're called? In what ways are you living out your identity as part of a royal priesthood?

Prayer: Holy God, who clothes us in righteousness and calls us to serve, help us to embrace our priestly role with the dignity, beauty, and devotion it deserves. May our lives reflect the intricate craft of your Spirit, and may we represent the concerns of our community before you with faithfulness and love. Empower us by the grace of Jesus, our high priest, to serve you and others with excellence and compassion. Amen.

Day 48

Together in Completion

Reading: Exodus 39:32-43

Exodus 39:32-43 marks the culmination of the tabernacle's construction, where every piece comes together, each thread, board, and curtain, culminating in a space worthy of God's presence. This completion isn't just about the physical structure. It's a testament to the community's obedience, unity, and dedication. The passage closes with Moses inspecting the work and blessing the people, a decisive moment of affirmation and consecration.

For our spiritual lives, this passage is a profound reminder of the importance of faithfulness in the small things. Just as the tabernacle was made up of countless individual pieces, each crafted with care and precision, so is our journey of faith made up of daily acts of obedience, small gestures of love, and consistent steps of growth. The completion of the tabernacle challenges us to see the beauty and significance in the routine and often overlooked aspects of our spiritual walk.

Exodus 39:32-43 also speaks to the value of community in God's work. The tabernacle wasn't built by one person but by a whole community, each contributing skills and resources. This reflects the nature of the church, a body of diverse individuals united in a common purpose. We are reminded that our spiritual lives are not solitary endeavors but are deeply interconnected with others. Our gifts, no matter how seemingly insignificant, are vital to the body's health and mission.

Moreover, this passage highlights the importance of accountability and blessing. Moses' inspection symbolizes the accountability we all need in our lives—people who can look at our work, our growth, and our character and offer critique and encouragement. His blessing represents the affirmation we all long for, a recognition that our efforts, done in obedience to God, are seen and valued.

Exodus 39:32–43 points us to Jesus, the one in whom all God's promises find their "Yes" and "Amen." In Christ, we see the perfect example of obedience, the ultimate builder of the church, and the one who blesses us with every spiritual blessing. Through Jesus, we can live with faithfulness, unity, and dedication, building up his body until we all reach fullness in him.

Big Idea: Value the small acts of faithfulness and unity that build up the body of Christ, seeking and offering accountability and blessing.

Reflection: What "small pieces" are you contributing to the work of God in your life and community? Who provides accountability in your spiritual journey, and how do you receive their feedback?

Prayer: God of Completion, who brings all things to fruition, help us to value the small acts of obedience and love that make up our spiritual lives. Strengthen our sense of community so that we might build up your body in unity and purpose. Bless our efforts, and may they be pleasing in your sight. Empower us through Jesus, in whose name we commit our work and lives. Amen.

Day 49

Dwelling in Devotion

Reading: Exodus 40:1–33

Exodus 40:1–33 portrays the culmination of the tabernacle's construction and its consecration. This isn't just the end of a building project; it's the beginning of God's dwelling among his people in a new and profound way. The meticulous instructions and obedient assembly underscore the sacredness of the space and the Divine presence that fills it. This passage doesn't merely recount historical facts. It invites us to a deeper understanding of God's desire to dwell among us.

For our spiritual lives, Exodus 40 serves as a reminder of the sanctity of God's presence and the importance of following his directions in our lives. Just as the tabernacle was set up according to God's specific instructions, we are also called to align our lives with God's will, understanding that he is the architect of our faith journey. Setting up the tabernacle piece by piece can be seen as a metaphor for spiritual growth—an intentional, gradual, and obedient process.

Furthermore, this passage highlights the theme of readiness. The Israelites had to be prepared for God's presence to fill the tabernacle. Similarly, we must prepare our hearts and minds daily for God's presence. This involves prayer, reading Scripture, confessing sins, and living out justice, love, and mercy in everyday interactions. It's about creating a space within ourselves and our communities where God's Spirit dwells and works.

Exodus 40:1–33 also speaks profoundly to how we should live as Christians. The themes of peace, justice, reconciliation, and love are woven throughout the narrative. The tabernacle was where people came to seek forgiveness and reconciliation with God, symbolizing the peace and restoration available to us. We are called to carry this peace and reconciliation in a broken world, reflecting God's love and compassion in our actions and relationships.

Moreover, this chapter points us to Jesus, the ultimate embodiment of God's presence among us. In Christ, the Word became flesh and tabernacled among us. Through Jesus, we can become a dwelling place for God's Spirit, carrying his presence wherever we go. Jesus embodies the grace, love, and obedience depicted in Exodus 40, showing us the way to live in alignment with God's will.

Big Idea: Prepare your heart as a sacred space for God, aligning your life with his will to manifest his presence and grace.

Reflection: How are you preparing yourself for God's presence in your life? What steps can you take to align your life more closely with God's will?

Prayer: Gracious God, who desires to dwell among your people, help us to prepare our hearts and lives for your presence. Guide us in obedience and humility so that we might create a space for you to work within us and through us. May our lives reflect the love and grace of Jesus, in whose name we strive to live and serve. Amen.

Day 50

Guided by Glory

Reading: Exodus 40:34-38

Exodus 40:34-38 presents a moment of awe and wonder as the cloud covers the Tent of Meeting, and the glory of the Lord fills the tabernacle. This passage symbolizes God's faithful presence among his people, guiding them through their journey. The cloud and the fire are not just ancient signs but represent the ongoing presence and guidance of God in the lives of believers.

This divine manifestation reminds us that God is not a distant deity but a present guide and provider for our spiritual lives. The cloud by day and fire by night were constant reminders to the Israelites of God's nearness and direction. Similarly, we must recognize and rely on God's presence in our daily journey. Just as the Israelites moved only when the cloud lifted, we, too, should seek God's timing and direction in all our decisions.

Exodus 40:34-38 also speaks profoundly to how we should live as Christians. The themes of peace, justice, and reconciliation are integral to following a God who guides and accompanies his people. As modern-day followers of Christ, we are called to discern and respond to God's presence and lead in our efforts to promote peace, enact justice, and live out reconciliation in a fractured world. This discernment requires humility and prayer, seeking God's will above our own.

Moreover, this passage invites us to consider our response to God's presence. Do we acknowledge and honor God's presence in our lives or ignore the divine guidance available to us? Awareness of God's presence should transform our actions, relationships, and beings.

Furthermore, Exodus 40:34–38 points us to Jesus, the ultimate manifestation of God's presence and glory. In Jesus Christ, the Word became flesh and made his dwelling among us. Through his life, death, and resurrection, Jesus embodies God's guiding presence, leading us into all truth and grace. His sacrificial love and enabling power equip us to be disciples who walk in step with God's Spirit.

Big Idea: Recognize and respond to God's guiding presence, embodying his love, peace, justice, and reconciliation in your journey.

Reflection: How are you attuning your life to God's presence and guidance? In what ways can you better recognize and respond to his direction?

Prayer: Ever-present God, who guided your people through cloud and fire, help us recognize and respond to your presence in our lives. Fill us with a deep awareness of your nearness and guide our steps toward love, hope, faith, peace, justice, and reconciliation. May our lives reflect the glory and grace of Jesus, in whose name we journey and serve. Amen.

Appendix 1

Daily Devotions with Jesus Devotional Books and Podcast

Daily Devotions with Jesus aims to help you dive deeply into the Bible, grow spiritually, and learn how to impact the world as a follower of Jesus Christ. After all, these devotions aren't just about learning about the Bible. They are also about growing ever more deeply in love with Jesus and following him with every fiber of your being and in every area of your life.

The Daily Devotions with Jesus devotional books and podcast offer a rich, engaging, and spiritually nourishing experience.

Podcast Links:

https://linktr.ee/dailydevotions
https://grahamjosephhill.com/devotions

Features:

The Daily Devotions with Jesus podcast offers a wide range of engaging and beneficial features:

1. **Daily Episodes:** Each episode, lasting 10–15 minutes, focuses on a specific Bible chapter or set of verses, offering a

Appendix 1

detailed exploration (moving through the entire Bible, from Genesis to Revelation).

2. **In-Depth Reflections:** Rev. Dr. Hill provides insightful reflections and interpretations of each chapter or set of verses, helping you understand the context and relevance of the Bible in modern life.

3. **Historical and Cultural Insights:** The podcast provides background information on the historical and cultural context of the Bible passage to enhance your understanding.

4. **Christian Practices:** Each episode prompts you to reflect on how you can put the Bible's themes into practice through peacemaking, compassion, mercy, humility, love, justice, reconciliation, and more.

5. **Questions for Reflection:** The podcast offers questions for reflection and prompts for journaling to deepen your engagement with the Bible.

6. **Guided Prayers:** Each episode integrates guided prayers tailored to the day's Bible reading, encouraging spiritual growth and personal reflection.

7. **Flexible Pace:** The podcast offers relaxed and flexible pacing, allowing you to delve deeper into each chapter or set of verses.

8. **Devotional Books:** You can also get the devotional books accompanying this podcast, which are excellent for individual and group study (see https://grahamjosephhill.com/books).

9. **Bible Reading Plan:** You can follow the Bible Reading Plan at https://grahamjosephhill.com/biblereadingplan.

10. **Listening Options:** To listen on a range of podcasting platforms see https://linktr.ee/dailydevotions.

Appendix 2

Bible Reading Plan

GrahamJosephHill.com/BibleReadingPlan

This Bible Reading Plan shows you how to read the entire Bible, exploring each chapter's themes in depth.

Each day you will read a chapter or set of verses and the devotional book dedicated to the book of the Bible you're reading and you can tune into the accompanying Daily Devotions with Jesus podcast episode.

Tips for Staying on Track:

1. **Keep the Goal in Mind:** The goal is to grow ever more deeply in love with Jesus and follow him with every fiber of your being and in every area of your life.
2. **Set a Specific Time:** Dedicate a specific time of the day to read and listen to the podcast episode.
3. **Reflect and Pray:** Take time to reflect on the chapter or set of verses and pray.
4. **Keep a Journal:** Note down your thoughts or insights from each day's reading.

5. **Seek Understanding:** If a chapter or set of verses are difficult to understand, consider consulting the Daily Devotions with Jesus devotional book dedicated to the book of the Bible you're reading.
6. **Stay Committed:** It's a long journey but staying committed will be rewarding.
7. **Explore the Bible with Others:** Discussing the Bible and devotions in groups can help keep you on track and make your experience more rewarding.
8. **Go Gentle on Yourself:** If you miss a day, go gentle on yourself. You can pick up reading tomorrow. Grace is at the heart of our relationship with Jesus.

The Bible Reading Plan

See the Bible Reading Plan at GrahamJosephHill/BibleReadingPlan. This will be updated as each book of the Bible is completed for the devotional books and podcast.

Appendix 3

Other Books and Resources by Graham Joseph Hill

Author and Ministry Websites

Linktr.ee/dailydevotions
GrahamJosephHill.com
TheGlobalChurchProject.com

Books

Healing Our Broken Humanity: Practices for Revitalizing the Church and Renewing the World. Downers Grove, IL: InterVarsity, 2018 (with Grace Ji-Sun Kim).

Hide This in Your Heart: Memorizing Scripture for Kingdom Impact. Colorado Springs, CO: NavPress, 2020 (with Michael Frost).

Holding Up Half the Sky: A Biblical Case for Women Leading and Teaching in the Church. Eugene, OR: Cascade, 2020.

Salt, Light, and a City, Second Edition: Conformation—Ecclesiology for the Global Missional Community: Volume 2, Majority World Voices. Eugene, OR: Cascade, 2020.

Salt, Light, and a City, Second Edition: Ecclesiology for the Global Missional Community: Volume 1, Western Voices. Eugene, OR: Cascade, 2017.

The Soul Online: Bereavement, Social Media, and Competent Care. Eugene, OR: Wipf and Stock, 2022 (with Desiree Geldenhuys).

Sunburnt Country, Sweeping Pains: The Experiences of Asian Australian Women in Ministry and Mission. Eugene, OR: Wipf and Stock, 2022.

World Christianity: An Introduction. Eugene, OR: Cascade, 2024.

www.ingramcontent.com/pod-product-compliance
Lightning Source LLC
Chambersburg PA
CBHW071729090426
42738CB00011B/2429